Catholics Coming Home

Catholics Coming Home

A Journey of Reconciliation

A Handbook for Churches Reaching
Out to Inactive Catholics

Carrie Kemp & Donald Pologruto, C.S.P.

 HarperSanFrancisco
A Division of HarperCollinsPublishers

FIRST EDITION

Library of Congress Cataloging-in-Publication Data

Kemp, Carrie.
    Catholics coming home : a journey of reconciliation : a handbook for churches reaching out to inactive Catholics / Carrie Kemp and Donald Pologruto — 1st ed.
        p.   cm.
    Includes bibliographical references and index.
    ISBN 0–06–066657-9 (pbk. : acid free):
    1. Evangelistic work — United States.   2. Catholic Church — United States — Membership.   3. Ex-church members — Catholic Church.   4. Ex-church members — United States.   I. Pologruto, Donald.   II. Title.
    BX2347.4.P64   1990
    259'.08822 — dc20   89-46458
                                                                              CIP

90 91 92 93 94 MCN 10 9 8 7 6 5 4 3 2 1

This edition is printed on acid-free paper that meets the American National Standards Institute Z39.48 Standard.

For my husband, my friend, and my soulmate, Gary.

Carrie Kemp

To the memory of my parents, Peter and Justine.

Donald Pologruto

CONTENTS

PREFACE

But who were these people of the Catholic church? They reached out to me with hearts full of acceptance and peace. I heard their voices singing songs full of love and forgiveness, healing and hope. They could see the good in me that I had become blind to long ago. In some way that I did not understand, the song of these people and their church and the music of my soul were bound together. I needed to explore this link so that I could either break it completely or reforge, rename, and reclaim it.

Seeker and friend,
NANCY MURZYN, 1989

We hope, through the pages of this book, to raise the consciousness of all who comprise the Catholic church in the United States about the plight of millions of people whose daily struggles include their alienation from the church. We call these people seekers.

Quite accidentally, in responding to the seekers' needs, we discovered that we were ministering to them. It is a simple ministry: we listen to their stories. And, in ministering to them, we continue to discover new insights about our own journeys of reconciliation.

There are three main parts to our ministry story. In Part One we will introduce you to the phenomenon of inactive Catholics, first by presenting statistical information about who they are and why they leave the church. Numbers, percentages, and categories, however, do not tell the story of alienation as it pertains to an individual Catholic's life. Therefore, we have devoted Chapter 2 to actual accounts of real, flesh-and-blood seekers. Although we have respectfully edited information that could reveal identities, these stories reveal the truth of this ministry, a truth much larger than numbers and sociological data.

In Part Two we introduce you to our model of ministry, how it began, and what we do. We have tried to present this information in a way that will enable you to begin your own outreach to inactive Catholics. Chapter 3 lays the groundwork, including formation of your ministry team, while Chapter 4 provides a nuts-and-bolts chronicle of what we do. In Chapter 5 you will find the issues that are raised at our sessions addressed from three perspectives: the seekers', the church's, and our own pastoral response. Our model of ministry demands an awareness and integration of all three perspectives; to do less would seriously impair the integrity of our commitment to the seekers and to the church. Thus, it becomes clear that in this model of ministry, the seeker and the minister learn from one another in an ongoing sharing of truth.

Finally in Part Three we challenge the church to become a reconciling community. We believe that in the process of facing its own woundedness, the church gains renewed energy and viability at all levels. Whether church is perceived to be the institutional structure, the parish community, or individual Catholics living out their baptism call to serve the Kingdom, ongoing reconciliation gives hope to the gospel message.

ACKNOWLEDGMENTS

Writing this book has been a difficult process for us; both our lives have changed drastically since we began. We live in different parts of the United States and have experienced ministry from varied life experience: Don as an ordained priest and I as a woman and lay minister. Our primary vocations have not allowed much time for our mutual avocation as writers. As a member of the Paulist Community, Don's days are filled with priestly duties and responsibilities to his Order. I am married, have a family, and a full-time job. I also completed a Pastoral Ministry Certification program during the time this book was being written. Our ministry and our writing had to be crowded into already full schedules. Therefore, we are grateful to the people in our lives who gave us encouragement and support when we needed it. Their confidence in us is what brought us to the finish line!

I thank especially my husband, Gary, who kept our household running so I could write and study; my children—Angie, Cindy, Greg, and Steve—for the joy they bring into my life on a daily basis; Dr. Ed Sellner; my theology professors, and the women and men at St. Catherine's College who helped me find words and the courage to answer my call to ministry. Finally I thank Don, who has been my friend throughout the agonizing process of finding the right words to tell our story.

Carrie Kemp

I am especially grateful to my brothers and their wives, Paul and Susan, David and Kathy, and to their families, who always offer me a place to come home to; to Kathryn Hampel, who walks with me in my journey toward God, to the Paulist Fathers who have continued to support our reconciliation ministry, and to Carrie and Gary Kemp for being my friends.

Donald Pologruto

Catholics
Coming Home

PART ONE

Chapter 1

INACTIVE CATHOLICS:
Why Some Leave and Others Return

A revolution of sorts is mounting in the Catholic church in the United States. Unlike revolutions that have throughout human history sought to overthrow one regime for another, this revolution seeks to restore, to mend, and to heal. The hopeful energy of this revolution is replacing the attitude of passive obedience that earmarked American Catholics of a generation ago. This is a revolution born in the hearts and souls of American Catholic laity who are no longer content to sit passively in the spectator section of the church arena. It is a confusing time to be a Catholic. While the word *Catholic* once conjured up images of certainty and authority, it has become a catalyst for argument, questioning, doubt, and insecurity. The church once considered to be all-knowing is being challenged daily by new information, new societal changes, new understandings of God. It is no longer a peaceful refuge. With Vatican II nearly a quarter of a century behind us, the Catholic church in America is struggling through an adolescence marked by turmoil, rebellion, confusion, and startling discoveries of its real identity and mission. While needing and longing to be connected with its parent church and the past, this offspring's true identity is rooted in the connectedness of its members to one another and in a common commitment to the sacredness of all life on this earth.

For those who do not see the signs of hope in this advent period of church, the result of this turmoil is alienation. In a very real sense, the victims of the revolution are those men and women whose Catholic heritage rests on a foundation of vague memories and fragmented truths. While they may be estranged from the church, they seek something deeper from life, something to replace confusion and insecurity with purpose and serenity. We call these victims "seekers" because of their courageous quest for an honest faith experience. Our ministry is an ongoing discovery of the relationship between the seekers and the Catholic church during this critical, unwritten period of church history. Over a period of several years, we have met with nearly a thousand seekers, sharing in their journeys, listening to their stories. While they are like us in their weakness, self-doubt, and sinfulness, they do not sit next to us in the pews on Sunday. They no longer celebrate the seasons of their lives within our Catholic faith communities. Most continue the quest for some semblance of compatibility with the church of their baptism.

We identify easily with the seekers. One of us is a Catholic priest whose struggles with the church culminated in parting from it completely during his college years. The other is a divorced, remarried Catholic woman who felt abandoned by her church when her twenty-two-year-old marriage ended. Our stories are commonplace in the American Catholic experience. What sets us apart is that we found our way back, not only to church, but to a totally new awareness of what it means to be Catholic. The ministry experience that we describe in this book began with a small effort to reach out to others whose lives were suspended in a spiritual limbo because of unresolved church issues.

In the beginning we were unaware of the sheer numbers of inactive Catholics. Various Gallup studies indicate there are more than fifteen million people who comprise this remnant of Catholic culture in America. In his book *Troubled Catholics,*

Bishop Norbert F. Gaughan states, "The second largest denomination [in the United States] is comprised of fallen away Catholics."[1] The staggering reality of these numbers has had a profound effect on what active Catholics perceive to be church.

The seekers are, after all, our parents, children, sisters, brothers, close friends, spouses. We know them at work; we meet them socially. Their status as "former" Catholics somehow reveals itself, although most choose not to discuss that status with those closest to them, especially not with their families. And so that unmentioned gap lies between us, preventing the very thing that makes us church: our connectedness to one another.

Whether we call ourselves the "one holy Catholic and apostolic church," the "people of God," or "the Body of Christ," church has come to mean all who have been baptized into the Catholic faith community. In its purely historical and universal sense, it means even more. Church is all of us. The rootedness of our faith in the lived experience of Jesus Christ demands that love, forgiveness, reconciliation, and celebration be offered to all; to exclude anyone is to impair the full promise of what church can be for the rest of us.

Almost as significant as the phenomenon of inactive Catholics itself is the growing interest among active Catholics to provide encouragement and hope for the seekers and for all of us who minister to them. Tandem to our work with the seekers is an ongoing interaction with active Catholics who want to know them, understand them, and invite them back. While older, more abstract concepts of church are being challenged, defended, and redefined by clergy and hierarchy, lay women and men especially are crying out for healing of the church's wounds—and they want to see that healing begin to happen now. This book is a response to that cry.

If you are an inactive Catholic, it is our prayer that these pages will offer you promise and resurrected hope in your faith journey, along with a new understanding of what it means to be Catholic.

This book is also intended for lay Catholics who want to make the road back easier for their inactive family members, neighbors, or friends. The deep interest and caring for inactive Catholics evidenced among active parish members is a continuing source of encouragement to us.

Perhaps you are a member of a pastoral staff, either in a parish or diocesan office. Some of you may be religious sisters or brothers; more of you are lay people. We trust that the ideas we present will help you to begin active outreach endeavors in your own community. We have tried to address those issues that come up most often in our meetings with professional church staff members, who include pastoral ministers, directors of religious education, adult education directors, RENEW leaders, RCIA catechists, and the endless list of dedicated men and women who work in the Catholic church today.

Our message reaches out also to priests and pastors, whose role in this evolving church is a vital and difficult one. It is you who represent the official church to the seekers; therefore, it is often to you personally that they look for the final word of reassurance and reconciliation. We hope this book will heighten your awareness of the seekers in your midst and the profound impact you have on their faith journeys.

Finally, we address this book to the bishops of the United States. One of our most powerful experiences of church occurred when one of you, in a diocesan forum, asked forgiveness from those who had left the church because of his offense or failure to minister with compassion. He cited several painful incidents where his zeal to be an "obedient priest" had overcome his call to represent Christ to the wounded.

No group of Catholics is exempt from responsibility for the pain that has been inflicted on these separated members of our church. Therefore each group must participate in the process of reconciliation. Lay people seem to be leading the effort toward open reconciliation with the seekers. That is not enough.

The Vatican II concept of church which stresses the entire body of Christ is unfamiliar to most seekers. Therefore the reconciliation efforts put forth by the laity are perceived as just that: on behalf of the laity. Again and again, the seekers ask, "Why don't the bishops say they are sorry?" It is time for all of us who consider ourselves church to acknowledge the seekers' pain and ask for their forgiveness. The absence of these good people must be noted and mourned in every parish. They deserve to be invited back. We pledge our efforts to heightened collaboration in the healing of this gaping wound in our church.

Before delving into our unique ministry experience, we invite readers to explore with us some data on inactive Catholics. One study, conducted by Dean Hoge of the Catholic University of America, catalogs responses from approximately six hundred Catholics who were recent converts, dropouts, and returnees. Hoge divides those who leave the church into two groups, according to age: those under twenty-three years of age and those who are older than twenty-three. His findings suggest that Catholics leave the church for the following reasons.[2]

Reasons People Drop Out	Under 23	Over 23
Tensions with the family	52%	2%
Problems with confession or personal moral issues	27%	15%
Church is boring	27%	24%
Problems with church's moral teachings	16%	26%
Spiritual void or emptiness in their lives	6%	22%
Changes/Mass	3%	19%

Hoge suggests that 42 percent of all Catholics dropout of the church sometime during their lives. He defines a dropout as a baptized Catholic who attends church not more than two times a year (apart from Christmas and Easter) and has been away from regular church attendance within the past three years.[3]

This same study also addressed the reasons that Catholics return to church. Hoge's findings suggest that returnees can be grouped into four categories:

Those who return at or before age 25	25%
Those who return at or before age 30	53%
Those who return between ages of 31 and 40	33%
Those who return after age 40	15%

Hoge gives the following reasons for people returning to the church:[4]

Why People Return	Percent
FAMILY LIFE (Out of concern for the religious upbringing of their small children, these individuals return to the church. One-third also have a spiritual motivation for returning.)	55%
SEEKERS (In seach of an answer to spiritual needs or from a sense of void or meaninglessness, these people return to the church.)	18%
GUILT FEELINGS (Because of a deep sense of guilt, individuals with a strong Catholic education return to the church.)	14%
MARRIAGE ISSUES (Influenced either by a spouse or relative, these individuals return out of concern for a marriage situation.)	8%

Hoge's study can be a helpful resource for anyone interested in knowing more about Catholics' attitudes toward church attendance or lack of participation.

Another valuable study is by J. Russell Hale, whose work was commissioned by the Glenmary Research Center in an effort to determine why Catholics leave the church. His conclusions classify inactive Catholics into ten different categories.[5]

BOXED IN: The church is too restraining or controlling for this group. Because they are constrained and prevented from growing by the church, they leave.

ANTI-INSTITUTIONALIST: The church is perceived to be too preoccupied with its own self-maintenance. It is too political, hierarchical, and removed from people.

LOCKED OUT: This group feels the pain of rejection or neglect by the church. For them, the church door has been barred shut.

COP OUT: Because their involvement was peripheral, this group was never really committed to the church.

BURNED OUT: All of the time and energy of this group was utterly consumed by the church.

HAPPY HEDONIST: The intent of this group was the pursuit of pleasure. Pleasure and church attendance do not go hand-in-hand.

NOMAD: Constant moving from place to place means no ties or roots for this group.

PILGRIM: These people are in a process of spiritual formation and have no direct ties to any church.

PUBLICAN: They define those who are in church as hypocrites, phonies, and fakes; therefore, they see no need to belong to the church.

SCANDALIZED: This group leaves because of dis-
unity in beliefs and doctrines.

UNBELIEVERS: Individuals in this group do not
believe in God.

The Hoge study and the Glenmary research project help il-
lustrate why people leave the church and, in Hoge's case, what
brings them back. Both are valuable resources for pastoral ministers, clergy, and laity who are interested in ministering to nonpracticing Catholics or who want to make parish communities
more inviting to them.

While the data and information provided by Hoge and Hale
provide clear insights into the inactive Catholic phenomenon,
our purpose is to present information that will help you to develop your own concepts or methods to meet the individual
needs of the seekers with whom you work. Because the following observations arise from working with people at various
points on their faith journeys, they should be considered from
a broad ministerial perspective. Any outreach effort to inactive
Catholics should focus primarily on the individual's faith journey, with no predetermined concept of what category the
seeker represents, or where that seeker's journey may or should
conclude.

While some seekers may initially come to us representing one
category, their journey may, and usually does, lead them to another. As they are able to let go of their anger and hurt, they are
likely to move from one category to another prior to any real
reconciliation.

Bored Catholics

In Hoge's study the percentage of Catholics who leave the
church because of boredom was significant. However, this is not
representative of our ministry experience. In fact, Bored Catholics would be our smallest group. As we describe our experience

in a later chapter, you will see that the seeker's response to our invitation is key to our particular ministry. We do not randomly canvass neighborhoods. People who have grown bored or apathetic toward church manifest very little interest in the church, in being Catholic themselves, or in resurrecting such interest. Given this lack of interest in anything related to church, they are not likely to notice our invitation to dialogue and if they do, they would probably not feel a need to respond. For many of these people, religion or church consists of memory lessons learned in childhood school experiences. Out of the school setting where they were told what to do and what to believe, they find little relationship between that experience and life itself.

They drift away from church because, for them, it is "history," something completed, part of their past. If their concepts of church and God were closely related during that childhood experience, this boredom could also lead them away from any real spiritual life. God, church, and school were all programmed, meaningless ritual for them, rather than actual faith experience. Church is really a nonissue for this group; it causes no discomfort for them and offers them nothing of interest. Perceived by some to be calloused and uncaring about the matter, they are sure that they have done the right thing. They simply see no need for the church to be part of their lives and feel thoroughly justified in detaching themselves from the church that they identify with their childhood training. These are often well-educated people with higher than average standards of living. In their work and in their recreation, they have grown accustomed to growth, competition, challenge, and ongoing stimuli — certainly not to boredom!

Until some event in their lives jars their religious apathy, these people are not likely to pursue reidentification with the Catholic church, or any other church. We do see some of these people when they begin to consider where their children will go to school or what kind of religious upbringing they will have.

With very little introspection or renewed interest in church, they simply want to duplicate their own childhood experience for their children and to promote for them a Catholic identity. The logical course of action would then be to put the children in a parochial school. We hear questions like, "Where can I find the best school for my kids, in a debt-free parish, with a forty-five-minute Sunday mass?" There is a bit of bravado, perhaps even defiance, in such an attitude. They do not want involvement in Catholic community; they simply want to perpetuate their heritage as painlessly as possible.

This group may also reconnect, although loosely, because of marriage, baptism of a child, or family death. During these times, the church provides a convenient, noninterfering sense of stability. Although they may consider themselves to be back in church, the relationship is minimal and void of deepened commitment or growth. This group sees church as a membership, an institution, perhaps even an identity. The concept of faith as a journey, of church as community, holds little attraction or interest for them.

There is another kind of Bored Catholic whom we are more apt to see: those who are concerned about the lack of enthusiasm within their local parish community. Many of these seekers have never formally left the church. When they do attend Sunday mass, however, the lack of excitement or personal fulfillment they experience there repels them. Repetitious prayers, homilies that do not speak to their personal needs, and the lack of meaningful involvement with fellow parishioners are some of the reasons given to us for the sense of boredom experienced by this group.

But because they were taught as children that the penalty for skipping mass was eternal damnation, they attend nonetheless. They feel trapped: do they continue to attend mass, even though it seems boring and irrelevant, or do they stop going to mass and jeopardize their salvation? Most find the decision too difficult to make and therefore choose not to deal with it on a conscious level. The issue is not resolved. Some gradually drift away from Sunday mass while others continue to attend regularly but do not participate in the life of the parish community at all. They simply sit in the pews every Sunday. The unresolved issue gets buried deeper or erupts in angry frustration.

This latter group of Bored Catholics responds to our invitation, hoping to find some clear-cut direction about what they should do. They want to be a part of the Catholic community without the boredom and lack of excitement they have experienced there. They have difficulty making the necessary effort to change their unfulfilling church experience on their own. Most don't even know how to begin.

Many are convinced that our invitation to listen to them is their last chance to resolve this personal faith dilemma. They share their frustration and confusion openly, looking to us for a solution that will make the church, the mass, and Christian community less tiring and more meaningful for their lives.

These individuals can be the most difficult to advise. They usually want clear, black-and-white answers to the question "How can I be a good Catholic?" They were taught at a very young age in Catholic school what was right and what was wrong. Now many live with the anxiety of being "bad" Catholics because they are bored or uninterested in what the church has to offer them. But they want absolutes and guarantees, and we cannot give them what they want.

It is almost impossible to alleviate the effects of all their years of stored-up Catholic guilt. To tell these seekers to stop going to church if they are bored creates even more conflict, although it can be detrimental to any hope of reconciliation to continually subject oneself to the very environment that causes the alienation. In some situations we offer the option of regular church participation only if it is a positive and faith-nurturing experience. If Sunday mass has become an occasion of tension, anger, or frustration for them, we support their staying at home for a while on Sundays, while they seek some additional counsel.

They may need to distance themselves somewhat from the problem in order to gain a new, fresh perspective.

For others we suggest "church shopping." If their concept of church has been formed by boring and unfulfilling liturgies in their local parish, we do not hesitate to suggest that seekers try other Catholic parishes. We encourage them to search actively until they find a congregation that offers an environment that is comfortable and stimulating for them. Until they find that parish community, they are unlikely to ever become more than Sunday Catholics.

For other Bored Catholics, the appropriate course of action may be education that will bring them to a clearer understanding of Catholic teaching. That may mean starting over from the beginning. Relearning and reexperiencing what it means to be an adult Catholic may propel the seekers into an entirely new appreciation for the church and its relevancy to their lives. Rather than an obligatory experience to be endured every Sunday, mass finally becomes a way of celebrating that new appreciation.

To gain this deeper awareness and fuller participation in Catholic life, we encourage the exploration of fundamental questions: What is a sacrament? Why do Catholics go to mass? This seemingly simply, obvious approach is significant only because it is so seldom offered to Catholics who want to seriously explore their faith experience, whether they are inactive or not.

With renewed education and understanding of Catholicism, many Bored Catholics feel less inhibited about embarking on a more participatory faith life within the church. They begin to discover new concepts of what it means to be Catholic and a desire to worship with other Catholics. Even more important, they begin to recognize that this is a process that requires prayer, dialogue, and perseverance. Many find this experience of renewed faith expression challenging and fulfilling.

As ministers we help Bored Catholics find a parish where they will feel a sense of belonging. More important than a nearby religious home is a community that will challenge, support, and nourish them, spiritually and intellectually. When a seeker finds such a faith community, being a Catholic will never again be boring.

Searching Catholics

A larger number of Catholics we meet through our ministry are Searching Catholics. Already free of some of the absolutes they were taught as children, they are searching for a new and deeper level of faith. Hoge describes people in this group as experiencing a spiritual void or emptiness in their lives. The men and women we meet who comprise this group have a strong faith in God and a personal relationship with Jesus. Their organized, denominational Catholicism has been replaced by a faith centered on Jesus Christ by the time they come to us. They are often doubtful that their new spirituality can exist or be nourished in the Catholic church.

This is the group that views the church solely as a hierarchical institution. The heightened spiritual dimension is not present in the Catholic church for them. They see the structures within the Catholic church as concerned with raising funds, protecting old rules, supporting schools, and maintaining social organizations. Faith-oriented goals such as prayer, Scripture sharing, and basic theological and spiritual education took on a secondary importance in their Catholic experience.

The journeys of many of these Searching Catholics have already taken them to other denominations that appear to be less judgmental and that offer participation in more honest accord with their strong, personal faith. To them the ideal faith community is one that focuses primarily on the teachings of Jesus found in Scripture, rather than one consumed with fostering traditional and institutional needs. It is also a faith community that encourages them to question and explore answers, one that gives them room to change and grow as their spirituality develops. For them being a mature Christian requires new insights and discernment reflective of their lived experience.

For some the spiritual home in another denomination is a permanent one, and their faith search is ended. But for most it is only a temporary solution at best. Those drawn to fundamentalist and evangelical denominations often encounter a lot of criticism directed toward the Catholic church, a discounting of everything Catholic that sometimes challenges what, at some level, is still very much a part of the seekers' lives and faith identities. Depending upon their reasons for being outside the church, this can and does backfire and becomes the impetus for them to start taking another look at their Catholic identity.

For these Searching Catholics there seems to be a need, before permanently turning their backs on their Catholic roots, to ask themselves whether they missed something that may have been in the church after all. They need to explore that. At this point the seekers are very open and honest with us; yet they are apt to be cautious and perhaps even a little resentful that they missed some vital ingredient in their Catholic upbringing.

Searching Catholics become real participants early in the reconciliation process. They are accustomed to inner reflection and want to talk with Catholics who have strong personal faith commitments. They relate to the serenity and peace in the lives of Catholics who have a strong faith in a loving God, rooted in a personal relationship with Jesus Christ. Although they cannot remember that focus in their own Catholic experience, they are curious about whether or not it might be there for them now.

Others in this group look for God on their own. They have many good questions and they are looking for the right answers. They see no merit in organized church participation, so they leave church completely and develop their own personal religion. They are moral people, who willingly give of their time and money for works of charity, while they continue the search. But their faith is a personal one; it is between God and them.

It seems that Searching Catholics often discover this deeper, personal faith through tragedy or brokenness in their lives. A death, separation, illness, loss of job, or a broken relationship may have caused them to reevaluate life, religion, and God. It is a difficult time for many as they reconsider all other aspects of their lives in order to accept and understand the changes confronting them. Almost all would be drawn to a church community that would assist, support, and challenge them in that discernment process.

Searching Catholics seem anxious, eager to find out once and for all whether the church can really be their spiritual home again. These are the people who have least difficulty with concepts of individual conscience, with consulting the church as a teaching directive along with Scripture and prayer. They are not looking for an organization that will tell them what to do for the rest of their lives. Because their faith is or has already developed in Jesus and they are looking for a way to express that in their church experience, they do not feel, as seekers in other categories may, that the church must mean one thing to everyone. They can allow for fallibility of leadership. It does not disturb them that priests may say different things in different parishes, nor that lay people may have differing views regarding matters of church.

People in this category often speak of their longing to find answers within the Catholic faith community. They tell us that they regularly skim the pages of the religion section of the weekend newspaper, looking for a place to continue the search. They readily spot anything pertaining to the Catholic church because of their cultural heritage or perhaps because of a need to rediscover their childhood roots. Many are tired of searching and long for a place where they can share their faith in Jesus, but where they can also find spiritual rest and peace. There seems to be an underlying hope in the hearts of these Searchers that the Catholic church can and will be the place they have been looking for.

While it may seem too great a task for the church to satisfy the varied needs of those Catholics who are searching for a new and deeper experience of God, many tell us that they are willing to settle for a lot less. If there is even the smallest effort by the church to provide the support that is needed, many are willing to take another look at church. The fact that so many respond to our advertisements tells us that they are always willing to give the church another chance.

Our sharing sessions become a resting place for many who are searching. We apply no pressure and present no agenda. Instead we offer an open invitation to talk and to share. We allow seekers space and provide encouragement as we discuss what it means to search for God and to worship God in a community we call home.

Since the seekers form the agenda at our meetings, they seem to feel comfortable asking the questions that have plagued them for a long time. The sessions are an important step in the long journey toward personal discernment of spiritual truth. They tell us it is just what they have been searching for: a setting within the Catholic church that not only allows but invites them to discuss issues that are paramount to their struggle for a more meaningful relationship with God, a struggle that includes a sense of direction as they try to fit together the complex pieces of their lives.

It is helpful for these Searching Catholics to meet others in the group who are searching. They offer one another support and affirmation. These are the people most likely to ask for private conversations with team members. For this group especially, we always have names and telephone numbers of counselors, spiritual directors, and other professionals who can help them in the search process.

This is the group that may be very ready to reconcile, and when they do, they seem to plug into church in a committed, healthy way, not just out of obligation. Our process is only the first step, but if that first step is a positive one, seekers in this general category are likely to continue their journeys of reconciliation.

Angry Catholics

A large number of seekers who come to our sessions are Angry Catholics. These are the people in Hale's study who are described as "locked out," "anti-institutionalists," and "scandalized." Their anger is mixed with lots of confusion about many issues. For many, life experiences have caused their break with the church. They have not had an opportunity to scrutinize their anger enough to know exactly where it should rest; the church becomes the logical target.

Many Angry Catholics are more than angry; they are anti-Catholic as well. While some inactive Catholics simply feel banished from the church or feel rejected by it, these people are vocal and energetic about their anti-Catholic feelings. Rather than subsiding during their time away from the church, their anger seems to have mounted. Somehow their identity is defined in terms of their anti-Catholic status. By the time they come to our sessions, they are ready to explode.

These people respond with hostility to most of the church's teachings—confession, interpretation of laws, and required obedience. They eagerly relate problems they have had with clergy, religious, and Catholic laity. In spite of their intense anger and the fact that they have stopped attending mass, they continue to call themselves Catholics. Their inner conflict continues to rage.

Angry Catholics want nothing more than a place to vent all that anger. They want to discuss, perhaps even argue, with representatives of the institution that has been insensitive and uncaring and thoughtless of them.

In retrospect Angry Catholics often tell us that once they saw our invitation in the newspaper, they couldn't wait to get there and let off steam. We were terrified of these people when we began offering our sessions. While they may still seem threatening, we now believe it is healthy for them to release the hostility and pain they have stored up for so long. In fact we consider this aspect of our process one of the most essential components in any ministry to inactive Catholics.

At our sharing sessions we see firsthand the pain, anger, and hostility that has been part of the church experience for so many. As ministers we have to stay in touch with this reality if we are to remain sensitive and compassionate to those outside the church. These Angry Catholics especially are looking for someone in the church who will listen to them and acknowledge their pain. The injustices they have experienced need to be validated as just that — injustices. They need to hear someone in the church validate the hurt the church has caused and to express sorrow for that hurt.

Seekers who can lash out at representatives of the church, sharing their anger in a group gathered as "church," and who hear church representatives respond with compassion and sorrow for their pain, tell us this is the first and most critical step in their journey toward healing. Once the anger has been released and directed toward the appropriate source, they can begin to reflect more objectively on their faith experience in and outside the church.

Perhaps more than any others, Angry Catholics need time. It is unrealistic to assume they can be rechanneled toward healthy church participation simply by attending a few meetings or by more educational classes. They literally need to heal. Sometimes this means painful exploration of family situations, relationships, and personal experiences. They also need and deserve unconditional acceptance. One of the greatest gifts we have received from a seeker is the simple comment, spoken by a young man who initially came to us in seething rage, "You have given me unconditional love." It has been more than three years since he first came to our sessions and he has not reconciled with the church. But the rage is gone, he has developed a wonderful sense of gentle humor about his Catholic roots, he can see new dimensions to some of the injustices imposed on him as a youngster, and his spirit has found peace. We enjoy comfortable visits with him, all of which focus on church. He has enriched our lives and tells us we have helped him through a difficult time in his own life.

Although unable to commit himself again to the church, he is able to respond to and accept those of us who minister in it. He is typical of those Angry Catholics who continue to be leery, afraid the church will hurt them again. The process of healing deep wounds in one's spirit cannot be rushed; some dare not even risk beginning. We are always struck by the courage of those who take that risk by coming to our sessions.

We believe the church, whether it is solely responsible for the pain or not, must be involved in a process that seeks to heal Angry Catholics. The church must offer the nonthreatening environment where these wounded people can share their hurt openly with others who will understand. As church representatives we cannot step back from their anger. It needs to be spoken. More important, the church must not be reluctant to acknowledge that its leaders and lay members have been the source of much of that pain.

The initial stages of healing can be very obvious in these angry seekers. Gone is the tense, irrationally angry person who desires to dominate the discussion. And in its place is a more relaxed person, one who is willing to listen to others tell of his or her pain, one who displays an uncanny desire to begin ministering to the others who are hurting.

For some this transformation happens on the first night. For others it may not happen for weeks or for months. The transformation will never take place unless seekers are given the opportunity to dilute their anger. Trust becomes a key ingredient in the reconciliation of these angry, hurt people. They must learn to trust that the church has changed; they may even want assurances that they will not be hurt by the church again. We have to make it clear that we cannot guarantee that. Aware of the possibility that it could, we help them recover enough faith in themselves so that they need never again subject themselves to abuse from the church or its representatives. Reconciliation begins when they see their own goodness and worth rooted in God's love, not measured by church rules and representatives.

Patience is another essential component of reconciliation for the Angry Catholics. Both the seeker and the church community must be patient with one another. The seeker recognizes that this is a process that cannot be hurried or rushed. More important, reconciliation or full and active participation in the church does not happen overnight. The Catholic community should not try to push or pull the seeker through this process. Instead the Angry Catholic must be given time to move through the process at his or her own pace. Some are able to move more quickly; most need much more time and pastoral care from the ministers.

It is also important to remember that healing does not always mean a return to active participation in the Catholic church. For some the pain is so intense that the best we can hope for is a healing of their scars, a healing that *cannot* take place if they return to the church. While they feel that it is safer to live with healed wounds outside of the church, they may acknowledge and express appreciation for the healing that has taken place and the fellowship that provided the framework for that healing. But their journey teaches them not to pursue any further reconnection with the church. And so they move on, stronger and more at peace with their God. They go with our friendship and our blessings.

Our ministry is not concerned with those who have left the Roman Catholic church and found inner peace and a sense of belonging to other Christian denominations. We speak for those who have no church home, those who, for reasons we will discuss later in this book, may have been away from the church for generations. Still, they pause when they are asked to complete a simple form that asks for their religious affiliation. They know that they used to call themselves Catholics but they feel uncertain about their right to claim that identity. Many choose to leave that space blank. That choice creates a twinge of discomfort in them because of the void that it reveals.

When we began our outreach to inactive Catholics in the winter of 1984, we envisioned a program of "warm fuzzies": we would welcome them, they would return to the church, and we'd all feel better about ourselves in the process. Our attitude may have been a carryover from the days when "lapsed Catholics" were considered to be spiritually negligent in some way. Their salvation status rested somewhere between the pagan babies and Protestants! Meager efforts to minister to them were motivated by a need to save their souls and put their salvation insecurities to rest. That is just not what our ministry turned out to be.

Instead we discovered that reconciling a broken relationship with the church is not terribly different from mending any other significant relationship. It takes time, commitment, honesty, and great risk if trust is to be renewed. Without that trust, the mending is only superficial, or temporary at best. However, if it is securely rooted, the renewed trust becomes the foundation for a faith exploration that grows and deepens. Rather than seeing reconciliation with the church as the goal, we suggest that the entire process be viewed as the beginning of a lifetime journey of faith and conversion for the seeker.

We stumbled on this ministry by accident after noticing that the adult inquiry classes held in our parish, St. Lawrence Catholic Church in Minneapolis, Minnesota, were beginning to consist of increasing numbers of former Catholics. Unlike others who had registered for the classes to learn about the Catholic faith in preparation for joining the church, these people knew a lot about the church already. Indeed most of them had considerable amounts of Catholic schooling.

In case after case, we heard the same message: these people were *not* ready for catechesis. What they really needed was a place to work through the root cause of their alienation. They each had a story to tell; they had personal pain that had neither healed nor been acknowledged, as well as large doses of unexpressed, smoldering anger that were preventing any real progress in their faith journeys.

We decided to invite these former Catholics to an open forum where the participants could provide their own agenda. They would choose the issues and the truths to be discussed, both theirs and the church's. We promised them that that meant anything and everything they wanted to say about the church. Wanting to make a clear distinction from the customary classroom/lecture atmosphere, we called that first format a sharing session.

Only eight people came to that first session, but it was a session full of honesty, energy, and sincerity. The seekers did most of the talking. We left after three hours with a deepened respect for these people who were pursuing a relationship with the church in spite of deep hurts and unmet needs. We had felt very uncomfortable during those three hours; it was already evident that reconciliation with the church for this group would require more than a "welcome back" attitude on our part. It was the beginning of our realization that "warm fuzzies" were not to be our payoff if we stayed in this ministry, for the church has much to atone for in the alienation of many of its members. We felt compelled, on that night and hundreds of times since, to say on behalf of the church, "We're sorry." What is so touching is how willing the seekers are to forgive once they hear those words.

Two more pilot meetings were scheduled during that winter and the same kind of atmosphere was evident at each, confirming our growing awareness that these people needed a format in which acceptance and openness prevailed. An unexpected rapport between the participants and those of us who represented the parish developed.

As committed Catholics we had never before witnessed people so caught in the turmoil of a faith struggle, nor had we witnessed the healing power of Jesus Christ in such profound ways. Through acceptance, the honest sharing of hurts and doubts, and gentle invitations to participate in community liturgies, these people began to open up to his presence in their lives and in the church.

It was not our intent in the beginning to expand our program beyond our own parish boundaries. But as each of our three pilot groups met with us, we began to realize that the participants represented thousands more in our archdiocese. Over and over we were challenged, "Why isn't this being done on a continuing basis? Where else can we go to talk about these issues so freely? What about all the others like us out there?"

It was those first seekers who encouraged us to schedule an open session on March 29, 1984. It was their suggestion that we advertise in the Minneapolis-St. Paul secular newspapers. Almost doubting the wisdom of that decision, we decided to augment our publicity by notifying archdiocesan pastors that the session would take place, inviting them to place our ad in parish bulletins. We were pleasantly surprised to discover that many pastors chose to support our efforts, in spite of the fact that we did not camouflage our intent with pious or veiled phrases. We specifically directed our invitation to Catholics who were angry at the church for whatever reason and promised that we would listen to their stories.

As we nervously prepared for that first open session, our most optimistic attendance projections centered around the number twenty-five. However, we quietly assured one another than even if only three or four came, that would be the number the Spirit wanted us to work with. By evening we tried to shore up our waning confidence by self-consciously arranging twelve chairs in a circle that we had to expand again and again as we greeted more than sixty people who came from all over the archdiocese.

Our initial fear that a large group would stifle the open sharing we had experienced during the pilot program went unfounded. These people, whose names we did not solicit and
who had never been a part of our parish community or its programs, opened their hearts to us with a brutal honesty that
touched our very souls.

At the conclusion of that first open session, we were emotion-
ally exhausted but spiritually exhilarated. Not only did the
group open itself up to us but to one another as well, with a
sense of community developing before the evening's end. For
most it was their first Catholic experience of acceptance and
support. Certainly it was the first time any of them had dared
speak so openly about their grievances with the church.

Because the response to that first session was so overwhelming, we scheduled two more sessions to be held during the following two months. The intensity of response was repeated
each time. We were deeply touched by what was unfolding and
began to question our sense of direction. Our own faith commitment grew through the heightened awareness of the power
of the Holy Spirit to lead and direct us to look more closely and
respond more deeply to this lost treasure on which we had
stumbled so accidentally.

We continued to schedule sessions each month during that
first year, each leaving us more deeply moved by the directness
and honesty of the participants. Always they revealed a common intensity of anger, alienation, and pain, not only to us but
also to one another. The pain was more than anger and bitterness. These were good people who were hurting and the church
had not responded to their hurt.

We have never grown accustomed to the depth of honesty
and pain evident at the sessions, but we have developed a deep
reverence for it. Such honesty is not common elsewhere in our
lives. As the ministry more fully penetrates our entire existence,
our tolerance for idle conversation and self-delusion diminishes.
This experience has challenged and changed us, forced us to

look at our own faith journeys with the same brutal honesty the seekers bring to theirs.

As each of the sessions closed during that first year, we were alternately thanked profoundly for allowing the seekers to vent and then chastised because we weren't doing more. "We" became the church in the most personal, authentic sense.

By 1985 it was obvious that the seekers deserved more than a "one-night stand." They needed more time to explore the wounds that were opened wide during those first sessions. We discovered that our unconditional listening during that one short evening had begun to open most of the seekers up to the possibility of continued searching. It seemed unjust not to offer them more, so that year we expanded our program to a series of three sessions.

During those early months of 1985 we became aware that, if we were to accept the seekers' challenge to really allow them to explore the influence the church had been on their lives, we would find ourselves involved in something bigger and deeper than any of us had anticipated. This was no longer a small parish volunteer venture in outreach. This was ministry and it would change our lives.

Chapter 2

THE SEEKERS:
Six Stories of Reconciliation

More than polls or studies, we consider the actual lived stories of our seekers to be the real lessons to all who strive to understand why so many have either left or been shut out from the church. These shared stories have taught us the most about our broken relationships with one another. They also affirm that reconciliation is possible for most seekers and that most seekers are forgiving and understanding of the church.

Consider for a moment the labels used to describe people who have left the Catholic church: "lapsed," "former," "fallen-aways," "nonpracticing," "backsliders." We've even heard the term "black sheep" applied to those who have left our ranks. Many active Catholics assume that those who leave the church have no relationship with God at all. Further it is often assumed that because they have made a choice to leave, their very salvation is questionable. Occasionally active Catholics tell us that we are wasting our time on these people, suggesting that they are not entitled to participate in the life of the church. Thankfully that attitude is changing and a deep desire prevails among those within the church to reach out and reconcile with those who no longer feel connected with it.

We have learned that although the seekers may not be actively involved in the church, most continue to be in relationship with God. For many that relationship actually begins and is deepened during the period they are "outside" the Catholic church. Those of us who remain in the pews must recognize that the faith discernment process is complicated and often painful for those who leave; frequently they tell us that they feel as if it is the church that has abandoned them, not they who have abandoned the church. Father Bill McKee, C.SS.R., says of the seekers, "As prophets, they are calling attention to abuses or evils in the church which should be remedied."[1] Father McKee's words sometimes make "faithful" Catholics uncomfortable.

We hope you will come to understand and appreciate the goodness of the seekers you will meet in this chapter. We have gathered these stories over a number of years. The men and women you will meet are of varying ages, backgrounds, and life experiences. All are honestly searching for a deeper experience of God. Although their journeys have been painful, they have risked sharing their experiences with us. All of them needed an invitation in order to approach the church again, to explore the possibility of reconciliation.

When we first met these seekers, we knew little about them. We asked only for first names and requested no background information. Initially the issues they raised concerning their alienation were not clearly defined. They did, however, focus on particular teachings or rules of the church. As we were to learn, the issues they brought to those early encounters were quite different from the actual causes of their alienation.

When we met Ed, he cited divorce and insensitive clergy as the causes for his isolation from the church. Margaret left the church when she married because her husband was Lutheran; that decision troubled her almost immediately. Al and Ruth were both divorced when they met. In spite of that, they married, knowing they would be at odds with the church. But they never gave up hope that one day the church would recognize their marriage.

Rick was a college student when he came to our session. He was challenged by evangelicals on campus and had no answers. He questioned his Catholic upbringing because it had taught him little about God, Scripture, or Jesus. Ann was a single woman who struggled to find a place where she belonged. Being single in the church is difficult enough, but being a woman in a male-dominated institution is even more isolating. Finally, Scott was not only angry at the church when we met him, he was also angry at his family. Issues revolving around his dysfunctional family continue.

The decision to come to a sharing session was only the first step toward reconciliation for each of these people. Except for one who has no desire to return, these seekers have been back in the church for three to five years. The intervening time has brought new dimensions to their lives and to their faith experience. Common to all the stories is the inner reflection that has characterized their faith journeys. Although they readily admit they don't have it "all together" yet, and probably never will, they seem more peaceful now, more comfortable with themselves, and more gentle in their approach to church issues that still concern them.

We selected these seekers because they are typical of many who find that the road back includes close scrutiny of their entire lives: their relationships, their families of origin, their marriages, their personal identities, and their self-esteem. It is not unusual, therefore, for a journey of reconciliation to reveal an entirely new way to approach life. It is a lifelong process of conversion.

In Chapter 1, we presented statistics gleaned from carefully prepared surveys and studies. The stories presented here contain the details of actual lives in and out of relationship with the church. They are beautiful, pain-filled stories, and they are not unique. Unfortunately we hear these stories over and over again. We hope this chapter will help you to understand how painful a broken relationship with the church can be. By telling these stories, we hope to dispel the litany of negative labels too frequently used to describe these people. In these stories we hope you will see a member of your family, a neighbor, co-worker, or perhaps, even yourself. What you will read is true, but because confidentiality is important, we present the information in a way that respects the privacy of the seekers. We are grateful to these people who have shared their stories and their lives with us so willingly.

Ed

Ed is fifty years old, one of those "salt of the earth" kinds of people who tends to sit quietly in a group. When he does speak, people listen because there is so much honesty, truth, and goodness in what he says. His unawareness of this gift makes it all the more powerful.

Born into an Italian immigrant family, the fifth son in a family of ten children, Ed cannot separate church from his strong family roots. Although they were poor economically, his father and mother tenaciously insisted that the family's security rested on its Catholic religion. Daily Lenten rosaries, May devotions, and daily mass permeated the family's life during the years that Ed was growing up and attending the neighborhood parochial school.

But religion made it hard for him to feel like a good person. The emphasis was always on what you had to do, and too much emphasis was placed on failing to do that. There was no freedom of choice and very little emphasis on personal goodness. Ed describes his experience this way: "You couldn't feel good about yourself just because you said the rosary every day because that was something you *should* do. . . . and besides, you broke at least one of the commandments every day anyway."

Not yet in his twenties, Ed married a girl from his neighborhood. Religion was automatically structured into their new life as it had been in their parents' lives, but it wasn't something they talked about together or incorporated freely into their relationship. Not until their first child died suddenly three days after birth did Ed begin the long process of questioning his faith.

The story of his daughter's death is a painful one for Ed and he has told it only a few times in the thirty years that have passed since it happened. He speaks haltingly and his anguish is clear as he recalls the event. In his grief, he was determined to bury his baby girl by himself and he made all the arrangements to do so. He carefully shaped a small casket out of a drawer in his brother's cabinet shop and gently wrapped the tiny body in silk handkerchiefs provided by his mother. He wanted to show the priest how well he had prepared his daughter for her burial, but Father wasn't interested and said, "Let's just get the show on the road."

At the cemetery Ed dug the grave while the priest looked on, impatient for him to finish. He remembers the priest's indifference and his thundering silence. It was a kind of violence that he would never forget. In disbelief he cried out, "Aren't you going to say any prayers?" The answer still rings in his ears: "Nah, she's just a little kid."

From that point on, the human connection between himself and church became meaningless for Ed; he felt no connection to that priest, nor to anyone else who represented church. He decided it would be better to pray directly to God than to consult a priest about anything that mattered to him. In retrospect Ed recognizes that he began leaving the church at that moment, but only inwardly. He shared the horror of that incident with no one.

Ten years later, Ed's marriage ended in divorce and the religious structure provided by the family wasn't there anymore. He felt isolated and alone when he attended mass at the parish where he had worshiped all his life. He explains, "At church, I felt like a fifth wheel; it was the divorce, but another thing too. I wasn't able to pin it down right away, but there was no fellowship." As the years passed, Ed found himself growing more and more alienated from the church while being drawn closer and closer to a kind, loving God. His personal experience of Jesus became deeper and stronger than it had ever been when church was a regular routine in his life. He returned to the daily rosary, not out of obligation or fear, but because of the peace those prayers brought him. Although Ed attended mass occasionally and still considered himself to be what he calls a "castaway Catholic," little remained of his Catholic background.

We affectionately call Ed one of our "retreads." When he came to his first sharing session, he was an Angry Catholic, still smarting from the isolation that his divorce had imposed on him. He saw no further need to open up the entire painful story again. He felt that going through the annulment process would demand that. Later he admitted he carried around a lot of guilt and resentment that seemed connected to church. Maybe it was better to just leave all his confusing feelings alone. He said little that first evening.

About a year later, Ed quietly took his seat at another session and expressed surprise that we remembered him. He seemed a little uncomfortable when he admitted he hadn't done anything about his church estrangement during his absence. This time, however, he had only one issue on which he wanted to focus: annulment. He was considering remarriage and was testing the waters one last time before deciding whether he would simply abandon the church altogether. "On the way to the session that night, I started worrying about whether I really had an excuse for an annulment and what you would say to me. In fact I remember trying to think of some excuse that would be the best one you ever heard! I didn't understand what an annulment was at all!"

Ed continued, "In a way, I was planning to do what I did so often: I wanted you people to know I was a good person, even though I had been divorced. But it wasn't necessary once I got there. I found out that it wasn't going to be like that with you, and that an annulment would involve writing down my history without condemning, but telling the truth as I knew it, and that my former wife would have a chance to do the same thing. For once we wouldn't have to blame each other. I really felt good about the things you people said there that night . . . it made sense to me!"

When he returned the following week, he had already made his first appointment with a representative of the Tribunal. By the end of the series, his annulment process was underway. All of this inner faith exploration began to flow over into other areas of Ed's life. He invited his fiancée, Carol, to attend not only our sharing sessions but a twelve-week education series as well. She seemed excited about this new dimension to their relationship and participated enthusiastically. Her decision to apply for annulment of her prior marriage was a happy surprise for Ed. As a couple, they became an inspiration to all of us.

But more growing and healing lay ahead for Carol and Ed. "There was a time," he said, "when Carol and I thought that if and when the church said everything was okay and we could get married in spite of our eight kids between us, and all of our problems, everything would be 'happily ever after.' That really wasn't true at all. I had thought for so long that being able to be married in the church would solve all of our problems."

So while waiting for their annulments, Ed and Carol also attended a Second Marriage Seminar sponsored by the Archdiocesan Office for Separated and Divorced. It was six weeks of intensive reflection on issues relating to marriage, relationships, communication, blending families, and intimacy. Through that course, they discovered more areas of their relationship that would require a lot of work if they were to face them honestly. Because of their new openness to one another, they began to risk more and more, sharing not only a deeper level of joy but also hidden areas of pain that had been sealed away by each of them.

It was a touching moment when Ed said sometime later, "I learned so much about myself during that time; I began to forgive myself for a lot of what happened in my first marriage.

Then I even began to forgive my first wife . . . to see things as they really were for both of us."

By the time their annulments arrived, Ed and Carol were so committed to working hard at being whole and healthy that they decided to postpone their wedding even further, until they were truly ready to enter a sacramental marriage. "Our concept of marriage changed completely," they explained. "We really knew what we were promising this time and wanted to make sure we could invite God to be a part of that promise."

About his own personal faith journey, Ed says, "The church used to say that if you don't believe everything it teaches, you might as well believe nothing. Now when I have questions or doubts, I don't worry too much about them. I know that as long as I have a solid relationship with Jesus, those worries and doubts don't have to be an obstacle. It isn't all or nothing for a Christian."

Life hasn't suddenly become easy for Ed and Carol. They have extended their honesty and their faith commitment to their children and families, working together on relationships that had been the source of discomfort in their lives. Their strong faith in an ever-loving God helps them through the hard spots.

In Ed's journey we discover God's gift of love and forgiveness. This middle-aged man came to know a new side of himself—a compassionate, nonjudgmental side. He could now forgive with ease not only those who had hurt him, including the church, but also himself for the hurt he had caused others. The church has truly reclaimed a lost treasure through reconciliation with this good man.

Margaret

"Deep down inside, I knew that eventually I would have to leave the church if I married him. Not because of rebellion against the church, but in order to have peace and harmony in my marriage." As Margaret looks back over her decision to leave the Catholic church, she feels that at age nineteen she was too young to understand the sacrifice she was making. In leaving the church, she had denied her Irish-Catholic heritage.

Margaret is forty-three now. She grew up on the East Coast where she was part of a comfortable, middle-class family that did not send its four children to parochial schools, but did see to it that they attended weekly religious education classes. Church and God were important but not discussed within the family. Together they observed the rules, prayed before meals, and ate fish on Fridays. Nothing more. Although they did not discuss religion with their children, her parents had strong spiritual beliefs that were deeply rooted in the Catholic church and their Irish ancestry.

"For me the church was going to mass on Sundays, wearing those cute little black veils, and going to confession. It was good, but our family did not have close ties with our parish priest or activities. It was a way of life and I never doubted that it was right for me."

But Margaret chose to give that way of life up shortly after her first child was born. Although he had signed all the "Catholic papers" at the time of their marriage, her husband would not allow the child to be baptized as a Catholic. Furthermore, he declared, their children would all be raised as Lutherans. Margaret could not imagine attending any church without her children. She rationalized that there was only one God and it didn't matter which way you worshiped; she chose to worship God as a Lutheran with her family. She tried to participate in the life of her new church community in order to make a permanent break with the Catholic church. She became involved in women's groups and took the children to Sunday school every week, while her husband chose to stay at home. She told no one at her new church of her Catholic roots. For fourteen years, Margaret told herself she was a Protestant.

Although she had freely chosen to leave the Catholic church, deep down inside she felt she had betrayed the church she loved, the church that had been good to her. She remembers attending Catholic weddings and funerals and feeling a self-imposed separation from her family of origin, especially from her three grandparents who had died during those fourteen years. At each of those funerals it had occurred to her that a priest would not bury her. Even more important, she could not be buried with her family.

It was uncomfortable for her to go back to her family's hometown, a small Irish settlement. The people there presumed she was Catholic because of her Irish name, her coloring, and her freckles. "I couldn't even go out there to a family reunion or to visit old relatives without all this being thrown in my face. No one else threw it up at me. I threw it up in my own face; it was right there in front of me all the time. I was the one who had thrown it all away."

Margaret had no one to share these feelings with. She could not even share them with her husband. A strain had developed in their marriage. Her longing to be back in the Catholic church and her husband's increasing use of alcohol were taking their toll. In an attempt to improve their relationship, she sought help from Al-Anon and the minister at their church. Both efforts resulted in an even greater strain on their marriage. She realized that her husband had a controlling influence on her and she needed to take care of herself: "I recognized that I had problems and needed to reach out because of them, but felt that in his church, I couldn't. I had no ties there. I felt that I had really goofed up my life when I left my church and I owed it to myself to find out if I could come back. It had taken me a lot of years to get to this point because I was so sure that those decisions I made as a teenager had locked me out of the church forever." Margaret was a Searching Catholic and her fear was real.

She considers carefully the words that describe her journey back: "I didn't come the first time I saw your ad. That church page was always the first one I looked at on Saturday mornings and I remember how that one Catholic invitation always stood out. But I ignored it for a while; then I'd find myself looking for it again. I still look for it! I was afraid to go because I was convinced it would be impossible for me to return after all those years away and [after] my heavy involvement in my husband's church. I really felt, even as I drove over there that night, that it would be the place where I would finally have to hear that it was too late for me.

"But I had to do something. I think about this sometimes: What if I had gone somewhere where they hadn't accepted me? I don't know what I would have done if I had gone to the wrong place, talked to the wrong priest, or if I hadn't been accepted so completely by all of you. That would have been the end. I wouldn't have reached out ever again. I know I would have felt that I deserved that and wouldn't have tried anymore. . . . I wonder what my life would be like today."

Margaret was one of those people whose silence and lack of participation in the group process revealed her pain. Everything about her that first evening said to us, "I can't belong here and it's my own fault." It was as if she had no hope of ever again "righting" the wrong choices she had made. She left without revealing her issue that first night. Several months passed before we saw her again. She explains, "I finally decided that I had to risk returning and finding out once and for all. I had gone to mass a few times after that first session but felt too much anxiety about even hoping I could return."

Her sparkling eyes fill with tears and she lets them flow. "The second time was so painful for me. It was the first time in all those years that I had ever talked to anyone about how I felt about leaving the church. I don't think I could have done it in a local church where people knew me. It would have been impossible if I hadn't felt anonymous at your sessions."

The sparkle returns to her eyes and her words quicken: "After each meeting with you, I would go home and pray so hard. I hadn't been very good about praying during those last few years, but I actually started having conversations with God! I couldn't believe how quickly the answers to all those difficult questions started to come."

Several weeks after the series ended and after one-to-one meetings with both of us, Margaret called to make an appointment to celebrate the Sacrament of Reconciliation. On Easter Sunday, she received the Eucharist for the first time in almost fourteen years.

Her life hasn't simply fallen into place since that time. Once the strong focus on the church issue was removed, Margaret was forced to look more objectively at the rest of her life. She and her husband have begun counseling in order to work on the marriage itself. And she sheds tears when she recalls that her father died not knowing that she had returned to the church. "It would have made him so happy."

She has been back in the church for nearly four years and has found it to be more open, more comfortable than the church she remembered: "I feel so good when I go to mass now; it is as if I am at home in the Catholic church. It is my connection with God. I really enjoy it. I actually pray every time I am there that I will never take it for granted again. Some people probably wouldn't understand that, but my faith means so much more to me now."

At the close of a weekend retreat a short time ago, Margaret's Irish face was glowing, freckles and all. She had reveled in the nurturing atmosphere that permeated the weekend: "It's as if they are mothering us . . . church really is a mother!" She noted further, with some surprise, that since her return to the church she has been drawn more and more to people who have a deeply developed spirituality, regardless of their denomination. She is surprised because she, who could never talk about God to anyone, now finds herself readily sharing her own faith experience with others.

Margaret's deep spirituality is already a gift to the church she thought would never again welcome her. Her awareness of that embarrasses and surprises her; it does not surprise us. Margaret is a saint.

Al and Ruth

The story of Al and Ruth is not very different from the stories we hear from those Catholics who have been shut out of the church for generations. These two have lived together as husband and wife for nearly forty years. They are deeply devoted to one another and share an uncomplicated, trusting faith in God.

Al's age—almost eighty years—has not diminished his tall stature, handsome face, and deep sense of caring for Ruth. At age seventy-seven, she is a tiny woman who takes pride in her appearance and speaks with childlike honesty. Years of shared joys and hardships have entwined their lives so deeply that one will often finish a sentence begun by the other.

They both come from German Catholic backgrounds. Al describes his experience of church: "Everything was German except the mass itself; that was in Latin. The sermon was in German, but I could understand that. I still speak German."

Ruth's church experience was different. When her father was killed in World War I, she was sent to live with Baptist relatives. She has mixed memories of those years. There was a lot of hellfire and brimstone and condemning of other churches. But she fondly remembers the Sunday school Bible stories that introduced her to Jesus. In comparing the two churches, Ruth says, "The Catholic church was special to me; it seemed like we had to be more holy. I liked going to the Catholic church although it was very strict. The priests and sisters weren't too kind, but they weren't mean either. I was kind of a bugger back then myself—a rebel is what Al always calls me."

Both Al and Ruth had been divorced when they met one another. Al had married for the first time when he was nineteen. The marriage took place in the Catholic church and lasted only seven years. Ruth had also married in the Catholic church at the age of sixteen; her marriage lasted nineteen years. Both continued to practice their Catholic faith after they were divorced, right up to the day they were married in 1940.

Ironically, it was their love and respect for the church and its laws that caused them to leave, even though it was a wrenching experience for them. "We stopped going the day we got married and never went back. We read all the time that you weren't supposed to be in the church anymore, but we never talked to a priest about that. We kept praying and hoping that the church would loosen up." Although they did not feel entitled to attend mass, they retained their Catholic identity during all those years. In 1964 Al was in the hospital and was asked what religion he was. He recalls, "I said I was Catholic because I always felt that we were Catholic, but when the priest came into my room and found out that we had been divorced and remarried, he gave us a tongue lashing." Ruth added, "Poor Al wasn't completely out of the anesthetic yet, so the priest really lit into me! He told me that we were living in sin. I felt like I was dirt under his feet. But I didn't believe what he said."

It was our little ad on the Saturday church page of a secular newspaper that caught their attention. Ruth was the first to see it: "I always look at the church page to see if there is anything about the Catholics—what the pope says, what is coming up new. It was such a tiny ad," her voice trails off as she remembers. Al adds, "If I had seen the ad instead of Ruth, I would have shown it to her. It was always on our minds and we both wanted to see what could be done. She sure didn't have to push me!" Both Al and Ruth were Searching Catholics.

Throughout the almost half-century of their marriage, these two looked for reasons to be hopeful that the church would change so they could be part of it again. Although they do not recall being apprehensive about coming to that sharing session, they do remember being surprised "that you were so friendly to us. We weren't sure what you would think of us."

But not everyone in the church is as forgiving and accepting as Al and Ruth. Their return to the church provoked an unbelievably cruel encounter. Ruth's unusually cheerful face grows solemn as she tells the story: "We had gone through the whole program, plus all those instructions and counseling. Our marriage was blessed by the church. From that day on, we began to go to daily mass at the parish in our neighborhood. It's close enough so we can walk. At our age we don't like to drive, you know. But after several months, a lady in the neighborhood who goes to that church called me and said we shouldn't be going to communion because of our divorces. I explained everything to her and she said she couldn't accept that; it wasn't what the church teaches and we were a scandal. I felt so bad after that I couldn't go back to that church."

Picking up on her pain, Al quietly adds, "We never told anyone but you about this. We can't say anything bad about that lady because she is a good person and she means well. But we just wouldn't feel comfortable at that church anymore."

Again the forgiving attitude surfaces, their willingness to make the best of things, their refusal to harbor bitterness. "We were so glad we learned in those sessions that you don't have to go to the closest church and that it is okay to find a place where you feel accepted. We belong to a different church now and feel welcome there. We checked it out for a while though, before we registered."

They do not dwell on the fact that it is some distance from their home and Al's recent illness makes it almost impossible for them to drive to church anymore. Instead they make sure that on the days he is driven to the doctor, they can also attend a noon mass where they receive the Eucharist. With our encouragement, they have requested regular visits by a eucharistic minister who visits with them and helps them feel connected to their parish. Recently they attended anointing services there, finding spiritual and physical respite in the post-Vatican II restoration of the sacrament known to most of us as the "Last Rites."

It is Ruth who says, "I cried so hard when the priest laid his hands on us. I just could feel something so special about that."

In their honest simplicity, Al and Ruth say being back in the church has been a blessing to them. Al says, "I feel more secure now that we are connected with others who have the same belief as us. I wasn't worried about my salvation, but I feel it is better now that we are connected. In some sense we always felt like we belonged to the church no matter what, but it's different now. We belong!"

Ruth adds, "I think it has made us a lot better in some ways. And yet we weren't bad people before, because we did the best we could and lived by the rules of the church and Christ as much as we could. We weren't out to do any harm to anybody or be mean, but it is so wonderful now when someone asks us what religion we are and we don't have to explain all about the divorces and everything—." Al finishes her statement, "We just say we're Catholic!"

They truly have always been Catholic and they are an example for all of us who claim to be church. One cannot be in their presence very long without realizing the mutual love that flows between these two people and their God. It is we who have been blessed in the sharing of their journey of faith.

Rick

At twenty-one, Rick was not a typical college student. He came from a close, wealthy Catholic family. He got along well with his eight brothers and sisters and had great love and respect for his parents. As often as possible, he returned home for weekends or semester breaks to be with his family. One of the most important components of his family's life is the Catholic church. For Rick, growing up Catholic meant attending parochial school. For a long time, the family assumed he would attend the University of Notre Dame when he finished high school.

Rick's parents held the firm belief that it was the responsibility of the church to teach their children what it meant to be Catholic. Attending Sunday mass was an important family event, but the Catholic church, religion, God, or Jesus were not topics of discussion at home. The only time the family prayed together was before meals; that was simply a routine ritual.

So it was school that influenced most of Rick's experience and understanding of what it meant to be Catholic. He can recount many stories of what it was like to go to Catholic schools and claims to have had his share of red knuckles from being slapped with a ruler. Once a nun threw a book at him because he was talking during class. His most significant memories, however, come from what happened outside the classroom. When he wasn't in school, Rick was at a Catholic Youth Organization activity or some other school-sponsored event. He describes himself as a sports fanatic. He lived for sports. But it was hard for him to fit in. "I was a short, fat kid; fat enough not to be good at any of them, but I loved sports anyway and wanted to play so much."

Rick, who thinks his extra pounds and adolescent awkwardness prevented him from playing on the team, rationalizes, "They played only certain kids because the emphasis was on winning. The rest of us had to sit on the bench. We never got to play." Because the team, the coach, and the games were all an extension of what he perceived to be the Catholic church, Rick's feelings of rejection were closely related to his church experience. In his mind, the coach represented church; therefore the rejection was devastating to him. "Not being good enough to play contributed to a lack of self-confidence that still affected me when I was in high school. I was taller and thinner then, also faster and stronger than the other kids, but I had no confidence in myself so I didn't even go out for sports. Instead, I partied."

Being on the team no longer mattered to Rick. He found new interests, new friends, and new activities. His attachment to the church became less important, and he forgot about going to Notre Dame, choosing instead to attend the University of Minnesota. It was the first step toward his eventual break with the Catholic church. Away from home for the first time, Rick found college life new and exciting. His roommate's fundamentalist Christianity was a big surprise to him. "I didn't know what a Protestant was until I was a freshman in college. They were in our town, but we didn't associate with them. I can recall wondering why some of our neighbors weren't at church—I just assumed everyone was Catholic." Although his parochial education had included some church history, Rick remembers the classes as being boring and irrelevant. To him religion was just another classroom subject. Like many of his classmates, he paid little attention and doesn't think many of them acquired very sound religious education in school. "They threw all that heavy theological stuff at us. Then they would give us these big reference books or the Bible, and tell us to write a paper on something. I always copied, word for word, right out of those books and I always got A's, but I never learned anything. It just didn't apply to my life then."

But in college his fundamentalist roommate was asking Rick questions about church, the Bible, and Jesus. This time it wasn't so easy to provide the answers. He had none. The unrelenting questions wore down Rick's limited self-confidence and he began to verbalize many of the inconsistencies he had encountered in the Catholic church. "I had been taught that to be Catholic was to be perfect. My roommate was pointing out all kinds of imperfections in the church. I remembered the thing about sports and recalled teachers whose behavior was less than perfect. I discovered I had learned very little about God or Jesus. I couldn't think of one teacher whose life reflected what it meant to be a Christian—certainly not my coach's!"

Rick began to look at the church of his childhood from a new perspective. "Something was missing. I don't know what it was. I believed in God, but there was this huge void. That void is why I left the Catholic church." Rick became a fundamentalist Protestant. At his new church, he found fellowship, acceptance, and friendship. Church was now more than routine Sunday worship. This new church gathered three or four days a week and became the dominating force in his life. There were Bible studies, late night talks, and even basketball! Rick was beginning to find a place where he belonged. He was able to express a part of himself that came from that void, and through that experience, he was gaining self-confidence. "Suddenly I was growing like crazy—spiritually, personally, and socially. It was great, but only for a while."

We remember clearly that first session Rick attended nearly five years ago. It was unusual for anyone so young to approach our ministry, even though the university campus surrounded the parish. A tall, handsome, young man, Rick was uneasy with us and shied away from our attempts to welcome him. He was an Angry Catholic.

In retrospect he tells us that his fundamentalist friends had warned him not to come that evening, that "Satan would be present there." When he realized that the young man sitting next to him was a Catholic priest, he was sure they were right! Rick sat withdrawn, detached, and disinterested as the rest of the seekers shared stories of their own personal doubts, guilt, and anger. Finally he declared emphatically, "I'm not worried at all about my salvation; I've been born again. But the Catholic church is sending my parents to hell because it doesn't teach them about Jesus and the Bible." He seemed to be looking for an argument and remembers that he was hoping for one. Instead he was encouraged to go on, to talk about what he thought the Catholic church was all about. In that telling, without realizing it he was revealing his frustration and confusion. In a sense his story was a plea for help and direction.

Rick's fundamentalist group was bearing down on him, pressuring him to involve himself more and more deeply in the life of the denomination. He was being discouraged from visiting his parents or from even consulting them about some of the drastic changes that church members were proposing for his life. At stake was the group's "discernment" that he should not spend any time with his family at home that summer, but rather that he should immerse himself in their summer camp, where he could embrace his new faith more fully and exclusively.

Through this entire period of estrangement from the Catholic church, Rick's parents avoided denouncing his new faith, in spite of their deep hurt and serious reservations about the impact it was having on his life. Instead they consistently extended their love and acceptance to him. The more he denounced their faith, the more intensely they assured him of their love for him. It became impossible for him to believe these good, loving people were damned, in spite of what his fundamentalist friends kept telling him.

Rick's thoughts go back to that first session where, in the process of the group sharing, he heard members of the team refer gently to their own deeply committed faith in Jesus. "It was like someone pulled a light switch—I had no idea Catholics talked like that—or that they even knew what a personal faith commitment was." He was most surprised when one of the team members, a woman about his mother's age, talked about her own faith journey and the presence of Jesus in her life. It made him think about his mother and her faith and how he had never really asked her about her experience. He had judged her faith by what his new friends told him Catholics believe. Rick became uneasy; he grew quiet as the session drew to a close. That quiet turned to dread as he realized the group was going to close by reciting the Lord's Prayer together. But that moment of dread was transformed into a new beginning in his journey of faith. "Something happened to me during that prayer. Standing there in that circle, connected to all those people who had been so honest and open, hearing their voices praying to my Lord, I felt a part of all that." The fear of the Evil One was gone, replaced by overwhelming confusion.

It was only a day or two before Rick found an opportunity to call the rectory for an appointment. That appointment was the first of many. Realizing that he was typical of a growing number of Catholic college students, Rick was instrumental in beginning a faith-sharing group that centered on Bible study and fellowship, two characteristics that hold so much appeal in the fundamentalist groups. Through this new group experience, Rick learned for the first time the importance of Scripture in the life of the Catholic church. But now he learned a new way of considering Scripture, a very different way than the fundamentalist literal approach. He learned the Catholic approach, which focuses on original intent, historic context, and the overall message of salvation.

For Sunday worship, Rick discovered a Catholic community of believers who celebrated the Eucharist rather than attending mass out of obligation. Gradually his new Catholic experience replaced the church he remembered as being cold, rigid, and legalistic. There was a place for him and his strong personal faith in Jesus in the Catholic church after all. Rick began to feel a sense of freedom as he moved away from that intense group of fundamentalists who had been controlling his life and all his decisions through their harsh, judgmental concepts. "I find that I am less judgmental now; fundamentalists seemed to be judging everyone else all the time and I was into all that too, forever determining whether or not someone was *really* a Christian, or whether they could possibly be saved. It was bad news."

Rick graduated from college, worked as an accountant for two years, and has now enrolled in a Catholic law school. He lives out his faith life through various forms of community and church outreach. "I feel like I can keep growing for the rest of my life now. I am at a crossroad in my life. Actually, church is opening me up to other people, helping me to get closer to them. That's new for me. And I am easier on myself. I have begun to understand that no matter what mistakes I make, God still loves me. Sometimes I still blow it, but I know that God really does still love me." Although he still has difficulty with some church issues, Rick is glad to be back home in the Catholic church. He realizes that it is not perfect, nor are those who make up its membership. He's okay with that.

Rick's honesty and deep, committed faith have brought new insights to all of us. Perhaps as church, we should listen more closely to what our young people are saying they need from church. It is wrong to dismiss them so easily, simply because they haven't conformed to the church we know. We have to allow enough space within our parish communities for them to explore and discover their own spiritual truth. They need to carry out that exploration in an atmosphere of close, personal affirmation and acceptance from more traditional parishioners.

Ann

Ann was taught in parochial school that the worst thing she could do was leave the church. Still, she left. It was a difficult decision, but she felt compelled to do it in order to find inner peace and the freedom to make choices about her life.

Now in her thirties, she still feels her father's keen disappointment that she was not a son to carry on his name. The oldest of three girls, she grew up with a secret longing to fill that special place in his life that she would have been able to fill had she been born a boy. Ann's mother became a Catholic when she married into her husband's Polish Catholic family. Being Catholic meant following all the church traditions: daily rosary, May devotions, Sunday mass, holy days of obligation. Although her family was faithful to all the Catholic traditions, they never discussed God, nor what it meant to be Christian or Catholic. "God was a four-letter word, a subject we would never bring up at home. I didn't hear stories about Jesus. I didn't even know who Jesus was when I was a kid."

Most of Ann's religious influence came from her grandmother, whom she loved and admired. "My grandmother was nonjudgmental. More important, she loved and accepted me. I connected her with the church. To think of her was to think of the church." Nearly every Saturday, Ann and her grandmother cleaned the sanctuary of their small Polish church. She fondly remembers the smells, the candles, and the stained-glass windows. In that church, with her grandmother always nearby, Ann learned to appreciate mystery and believe in miracles.

But much of that changed when her grandmother died and the family began to worship at a large suburban parish. Without her grandmother and in an unfamiliar church setting, Ann felt alone and detached from the church and her family. She began to question the faith of her early childhood and she wondered whether anyone, even God, really loved and accepted her. She remembers feeling that the church was judging her "even by the clothes I wore as I walked to and from communion." Sunday morning became a torture for her. Her father forced the family to attend mass together, although he slept through much of the liturgy. "It was a joke, it was superficial, it was awful to be there."

When she began attending public schools rather than the small, safe parish school of her earlier childhood, Ann faced the stigma of "not really belonging" to the church the way the parochial school kids did. The wedge between her and the church grew wider when the pastor told her she could not be an altar server because she was a girl. In Ann's eyes, the church agreed with her father: she should have been a male. The church and God were a reinforcement of her father's disappointment in her. "The acceptance and love I had experienced through my grandmother was not what I experienced in the overall church at all." Now instead of mystery she found hard, fast rules. Instead of miracles, she found a system of reward and punishment. In place of theological discussion and inquiry, she found dogmas that reflected little understanding of human weakness or goodness.

By the time Ann went away to college, she was afraid to place her trust in a God or a church that could not even accept her female identity. The risk was not worth the frustration and anger—nor the pain. But there was also a price to pay in leaving.

In shutting off the church, she had to shut out those deep feelings of love and acceptance that her grandmother's faith had opened up to her. "It was as if a deep part of me had died and would never be there for me again," she recalls.

For the next sixteen years, her quest for that missing part of herself led her in many directions. It included personal relationships that seemed for a while to offer completeness and purpose to her life. But each time, the price she paid was to be less than honest, less herself, and more an image to meet someone else's needs. Again she concluded that it was her femaleness that stood in the way of her wholeness, her ability to feel good about herself or to experience God's love for her. She tried to find the answer in other religions and her struggle took her to more than twenty different churches. None of them provided any lasting peace and each new attempt fortified her belief that her relationship with God was only clouded by the judgment and rules that accompanied these church experiences. She tells us, "Somehow, I had to get past church to find God and my own spirituality. I knew I was searching for something and didn't even know what."

It was at this point in her journey that a friend began to talk to Ann about Jesus—a Jesus who loved her enough to die for her and to whom it made no difference if she was male or female. "I had never heard any of that stuff," Ann says. "I wanted to believe it, but it was hard. It opened a door and I tried to push it away. But I couldn't."

Ann chose to continue with the struggle and the search. She had to find out whether this loving Jesus could be a part of the Catholic church. She was directed to our ministry by a staff member at a local retreat house. Her primary focus that first evening was on women's issues and the church's outdated concept of the female role. A quiet person, she spoke softly in a voice that did not reveal the frustration she carried inside.

It was in the one-to-one visits that followed that Ann began to trust enough to give words to her spiritual confusion. After several of those visits, she stated with some surprise, "It really isn't just the women's issues; that has been a smoke screen for my real problem with the church. The real issue is my whole concept of God, myself, and just where do I, as a single person, fit in? It took a lot of risk to trust the church enough to find out whether or not I can fit in again."

That wasn't to say that women's issues didn't concern her, but she hadn't found a way to deal with those issues or any others within the church. So often it is in the telling of our stories that we begin to find our own answers. So it was with Ann. She continued through our program and made individual visits with both of us. She came to a turning point in her search when she enrolled in evening theology courses at a Catholic college. There she encountered a new segment of church and learned to appreciate the church's history as well as its sense of direction. She found an environment that encouraged her to think, to challenge, and to explore concepts and ideas regarding church and how it related to her life as a woman.

She describes this new phase of her journey: "For me, it is a radical change — from thinking of church as an institution and something very impersonal, to many different images of church. Church is something much broader to me now. I feel so connected to the people I am meeting along my way and I realize that they are church Because of that connection, I understand what it means to be part of the Body of Christ. The people who have listened to me and encouraged me reflect for me who Christ is and what we're all about as we try to build God's Kingdom on earth. The sessions opened up a process which I am still going through. The whole question of my spirituality has been opened up again and my concept of myself is changing all the time — for the better! I like being a woman!"

Ann has addressed a crucial issue in the church. How does the average parish address the needs and gifts of single adults? These men and women often feel that the church considers them only in the context of a transitional stage — not yet as complete as they will be when they marry. Even though the Catholic church has always taught that the single state is a vocation equal to marriage and priesthood, community experience rarely reflects that teaching. We need people like Ann to raise our consciousness so that we can recognize this gap. Whether or not she marries one day, she already possesses the talents, love, and desire to serve that will enhance any faith community.

Scott

Although every faith journey is unique, Scott's story helps us to understand an entire category of young adults who were raised in Catholic homes, Catholic schools, Catholic scout troops, Catholic neighborhoods. These are the people who questioned nothing. Their world was black and white and it was Catholic!

Scott's entire childhood was regimented by the church. However, he learned nothing of God's love, of self-love, or of the value of questioning. At age thirty-six, he has discovered that many of those black and white truths which he so passively accepted while growing up incorporate vast gray areas in the adult world.

He describes his earlier years: "Life was crazy at home. I couldn't separate a loving, caring Jesus from a father who abused my mother and me when he drank, a priest who made the confessional a torture chamber, and nuns who beat kids across the hand with a pointer. I remember one boy who had his mouth washed out with soap and a scrub brush because he swore on the playground. That was how I learned right and wrong." Most of his anger rests on the fact that he never questioned anything. Still bewildered by his blind acceptance, he observes, "There was no choice, no questioning, no one asked what we thought. Maybe when you grow up like that, you just rebel eventually."

His family consisted of his mother, father, and himself. The three of them lived in a home where God was never discussed, only obeyed. God was a powerful force to be obeyed. They followed all the Catholic rules: parochial schools for Scott through high school, Sunday and holy day mass attendance, and frequent confession. A harsh, judging God was enmeshed in everything for Scott, who felt shame when his father beat him and was terrified that he would incur the wrath of the nuns who taught him. As an adult, he cannot remember any signs of affection or caring demonstrated between his mother and father; they simply endured a marriage fraught with abuse. He remembers, with deep bitterness, his mother finally going to a priest for permission to divorce because of all the abuse. Scott was at home when she returned from the rectory, broken and defeated. His anger flares as he recalls that the priest told her that it was her "Catholic duty" to stay in the marriage and that she should "offer up her suffering." His parents recently passed their fiftieth anniversary with no acknowledgment of the event. His mother, meek and submissive after a lifetime of abuse, found enough strength to insist that any form of celebration would be hypocrisy.

In spite of his recently discovered anger, Scott still keeps a box of "all that Catholic stuff." In it is the book he used to study for altar boy preparation. He couldn't master the Latin and failed the test twice. The priest told him not to waste his time on another attempt; there were brighter boys who could serve. More shame. He has held on to the book and the shame, but he cannot understand why he did not challenge that priest. He questions everything now and can't understand why he questioned nothing then.

Scott's journey drew him to an Adult Children of Alcoholics group, where he was encouraged to question and he began to see the good in himself. It was a place where people of all faiths and life experiences could gather in acceptance and affirmation of one another. For him that group became church and it was within that context that he began to experience a loving, caring God, a God the group calls a Higher Power. Honesty was encouraged and trust was the bottom line. For the first time in his life, he learned that the abuse he had experienced was wrong, and he met others who were victims with similar scars.

Until he encountered Adult Children, Scott had continued the Catholic regimen imposed on him as a youngster without questioning its meaning. Suddenly, none of it made any sense to him; he abandoned all of the rules along with his fear of punishment as the prime motivator to do good. In their place, he began to know a God who forgave, who loved, who wanted people to love and forgive one another, a God who was gentle and understanding. In a touching moment, he describes one of his new images of God as "a warm, loving mother, who invites me to sit on her lap and let her hold me, just because she loves me." That image brings a rush of peace into a soul tormented with shame and anger, as he begins to glimpse God's goodness in the person of Jesus. Scott believes his own spirituality was conceived in those meetings.

Because he questions everything now, he dares to ask whether it is possible for a God of love to exist within the Catholic church. Can it offer him all those things he wanted so desperately as a child but only found outside the church as an adult? He weighs his bad memories against his longing to be accepted and affirmed by the source of so much pain in his life.

When we drove into the parking lot the night Scott attended his first session, we knew it wouldn't be an easy evening. A bumper sticker on the car parked next to ours declared, "RECOVERING CATHOLIC." It was Scott's car. He was enraged and defiant and held the church accountable for all of the unpleasantness in his life. To put it mildly, Scott was an Angry Catholic. But he had responded to our ad inviting him to discuss his anger and so we listened. To our surprise, he returned the following week, and the next. It was toward the end of the second session that we heard him assure one of the other participants that he had been filled with rage the first week but that some of that had dissipated. In itself that small concession was a triumph.

Anger often shuts down the processes that allow for new concepts or ways of looking at things. But Scott remained open, painful as it was for him. Sometimes it seemed as if he was daring us to walk away from him, to refuse to validate his pain. There was one moment, long after he had completed the series, when he sat in a group and suddenly blurted out more of his pain with a short preface of, "You probably won't want to have anything more to do with me after I say this." It seemed cruel for him to say that to us, after we had endured so much of his rage. But the little boy in him was defying us to reject him before he risked trusting us further. Impulsively the three of us who were in the room stood up and embraced him. We just held one another. Words were no longer necessary.

A bonding occurred at that moment that transcends church affiliation. That bonding has allowed Scott to speak freely with us on and off over the years that have passed since we first met. It has also given him the freedom to let go of a lot of the "shoulds" regarding whether or not he is Catholic and concentrate his focus on his relationship with God, where he does find peace and direction. We stay in touch through phone calls and an occasional Italian dinner. While the subject of church always comes up during these conversations, the anger is gone and Scott's life is moving in a healthy direction.

Recently he talked about the breakthrough in his faith journey that occurred simply because we listened to him and validated his experience. He said he has taken responsibility for moving beyond that point in his life now and that listening afforded him an opportunity to begin the healing that had to take place before he could move on. A while ago, Scott brought his "significant other" to visit us. We were amused by the fact that she was more alienated than Scott and that he was actually offering some positive observations about church. That we could recognize this and laugh together was proof that Scott has come a long way on his journey. That is a success story!

Key to rekindled interest in the church for Ed, Margaret, Al and Ruth, Rick, Ann, and Scott was a parish community that reached out to them and made them feel welcome during all phases of their reconciliation journeys. Even Scott, who has chosen not to reconnect with the church, felt free to make that decision within the context of a parish community that still welcomes his presence when he visits.

In light of these stories, we invite you to consider your parish community and whether these seekers could find a spiritual home there. Our next chapter will help you in that reflection.

PART TWO

Chapter 3

THE PARISH:
What Are You Bringing Them Home To?

Ideally each Catholic parish community should be a center of reconciliation and healing, a place where any baptized Catholic could find welcome support in his or her faith journey. Were the norm anywhere close to this ideal, we could simply recommend that outreach to inactive Catholics be centered in your local parish. Reality, however, is a long way from this ideal. In fact, our experience indicates that most parishes include in their membership many active Catholics who are angry at the church, who seldom attend mass, or who attend regularly but experience very little spiritual inspiration from their parish community. While these parishes may not be quite ready to sustain an active outreach, they are fertile seedbeds for evangelization within their own membership.

Programs, activities, and liturgies intended to reach out to inactive Catholics need to be rooted firmly in the actual experience of the parish community itself. It serves little purpose to invite people back to a community that is incapable of supporting the seekers on their journeys of reconciliation. It is, in fact, harmful to extend invitations of hospitality to all, if in reality the church doors are barred to some. Many active Catholics live out their lives in parishes where only successes are noted, presenting a narrow vision of life. Christian community must encourage and support people committed to honest growth through real human issues. Outreach activity that is simply laminated onto parish activities, without inward scrutiny and reflection, reveals itself to the seeker as placating and does not convey an atmosphere of trust and caring for the seeker. Too often such programs amount to "busy work," with little or no lasting results.

Therefore, when we are invited to meet with parish representatives who want to start ministry programs like ours, we usually respond to their initial question "How do we begin?" with our own question, "What are you inviting them back to?"

Sometimes the answer to our question reveals a parish fraught with strife, discord, or lethargy among the *active* members. Caught up in internal fighting and bickering, the liturgies in these parishes often reflect tension and an absence of joy. Our counsel in such cases is to begin by helping parishioners confront existing problems, talk openly about them, and learn more about one another in the process. Too often parish communities simulate dysfunctional families, where the hurts and misunderstandings of the past are buried by activity and controlled effort to avoid honest discussion about serious issues.

We have seen dramatic change take place in parishes that have accepted our invitation to begin reconciliation within, to structure gatherings where participants can openly share the residual pain of bygone eras of parish history. Whether it be the abrupt imposition of sanctuary changes immediately following Vatican II, a childhood school experience that permanently scarred self-esteem, alienation during time of divorce, or the loss of a beloved pastor whose struggle with the priesthood and the church had been shared by the community, these issues need to be aired. Too often pastors will counsel their parishioners to forget the past, begin a new day, and go on from there. Or worse yet, the issues troubling the hearts and minds of hundreds of parishioners are not even spoken, hanging like a dark cloud over every liturgy and parish gathering. We need not hide, out of shame, conflicts that arise within parish communities; rather, we need to resolve them in a Christian manner. The alternative is to allow permanent harm to the congregation.

We are always delighted to be invited back to parishes after they have committed themselves to inner renewal. What we see on our return visit, usually a year or two later, is a community filled with energy, enthusiasm, single purpose, and the bonding of members that is the trademark of true reconciliation. It is obvious that many parishes are ill-equipped to even begin the kind of effort that must take place before this kind of atmosphere exists in their own church family.

Of course there is no perfect parish: indeed, preparing someone for reentry to the church includes developing the awareness that church consists of people and people are imperfect. So where do we, as church, begin some kind of active outreach to inactive Catholics?

If your parish community would like to get started, there are three major steps to follow:

1. Developing a Welcoming Parish Atmosphere
2. Forming a Team
3. Getting the Word Out

Developing a Welcoming Parish Atmosphere

When inviting guests into our homes, we often make a mental inventory of our family's housekeeping and behavior patterns. We want the visitor to feel welcomed by all, comfortable, and at home. Sometimes we even do a little housecleaning. As parish communities, we need to engage in this same type of reflection before we begin inviting people in. If we are truly interested in practicing hospitality, the seekers' initial visits must be comfortable, accepting experiences that provide confidence and reassurance. That caring, inviting atmosphere in your parish needs to be present every Sunday, not just conjured up for specific events or occasions. It is an injustice to lure seekers into a parish with little or no pastoral concern for its members.

Returning to mass after years away can be traumatic. It takes courage to get that far in a journey of reconciliation. It takes faith for seekers to believe there is room for them in the church after all, and it takes forgiveness to put aside the hurt that may have caused the breach in the first place.

Our experience indicates that people rarely reactivate where they were first alienated. They need time to test the waters before risking attending mass among family and neighbors once again. If the root of alienation was a person or situation specific to their parish of origin, they may never return to that parish. It is sometimes better for them to begin anew, away from the unpleasant associations of their previous parish community. They may need assistance in seeking out a parish where they will feel untroubled by ghosts from the past. For this reason, many of the seekers who come to your program may belong, in an ecclesial sense, to another parish. This is one of many positive aspects of the Catholic church; although your parish boundaries may indicate otherwise, the seeker can feel a sense of belonging to church through participation in your liturgies and activities. They need to find positive worship experiences where old wounds won't be torn open by cold liturgies, bored participants, or homilies reflective of little joy or understanding of honest human struggle.

Attending mass again is usually the first public step in the reconciliation journey and therefore takes on great significance for the seeker. One who has devoted time, prayer, and energy to the reconciliation process has very likely learned to appreciate the mass as something more than a weekly obligation. It is important that the liturgy reflect this new understanding. Most of the people we see tell us they have tried and tried again to attend mass, but are confronted with so much anxiety or frustration or loneliness or anger that they finally stop trying.

Others have been locked into a pattern of avoiding mass

because of unpleasant confrontations with solicitous family members who are concerned about their salvation. Whether you are reaching out as a parish or as an individual to someone who has been away from the church for any period of time, we recommend only gentle invitations, not confrontations.

An essential component of a parish outreach program to inactive Catholics is the availability of good liturgical celebrations in a warm, inviting atmosphere and people to do the inviting. If the seekers feel no expectations regarding their participation or commitment, the burden of "what will others think?" is lifted. It is touching to watch people who have a sense of dread or terror about attending mass still willing to risk enough to accept our invitation to attend with us.

We encourage them to simply sit and observe, to participate only when it feels comfortable for them to do so. We ask them to allow the presence of Jesus in the gathered community to minister *to* them, to feel all right about taking what they need from the liturgy, the community, and from our God, who understands that we have needs. This is not the time to tell them about their responsibilities during the worship experience.

This gentle approach removes pressure, fortifies the trust between the seeker and team members, and allows the Holy Spirit to permeate the situation, which is another affirmation that you are not in this ministry alone.

We vividly recall a man in his early forties, well over six feet tall and weighing close to two-hundred-fifty pounds, who sat trembling like a frightened child between two members during his reentry mass. Now actively living out his Catholic faith, he reflects with some humor that that terrifying experience more than three years ago marked the beginning of his journey back. As the warmth and celebration penetrated his wall of fear, he began to realize a powerful presence of God in the church. Only this time it was loving, welcoming, compassionate God whose arms opened up wide enough to include him through the community gathered around him.

In the course of our ministry, we have been invited to parishes in many parts of the United States. It may come as a surprise to those who worship in the same church every Sunday that parishes take on distinct personalities that are clearly revealed to outsiders. Because of our work, we try to see each new parish experience through the eyes of a potential seeker, imagining it is our first time back in church in a long while. Perhaps it would be good for everyone to consider their parish in that light now and then. Here are some of the things you can do in order to convey an atmosphere of hospitality and acceptance in your parish:

Welcome Your Visitors

A greeting at the doorway by the celebrant and/or members of the parish can disarm even the most hesitant visitors. Certainly it provides a better first impression than being jostled through the door by grim-faced parishioners who simply want to get the whole thing over with, taking no note of those around them. Smiling faces, the willingness to move into the pews when newcomers arrive, the helpful sharing of hymnals and missalettes, and ushers who speak kindly and cheerfully all indicate that this is a community of believers, not just obligated members. The physical condition of the sanctuary itself is not nearly as important as these human indications of Christ's presence in our churches. How does your parish measure up so far?

Preliminary greetings from the lector or celebrant, including a welcome to visitors and newcomers, and information from the music minister about the hymns to be sung continue to convey hospitality and to put the worshipers at ease.

Since it is likely that inactive Catholics attend every mass in your parish, a sincere acknowledgment of that fact, along with an invitation to make your parish their home, may be all a seeker needs to come back for another visit. We especially encourage this kind of acknowledgment and invitation during the Easter and Christmas seasons. Too often, inactive Catholics who attend mass during those times are met with sarcasm or belittling humor calling attention to their absence during the rest of the year. If we are truly a welcoming church, our message would instead be one of pure pleasure that they are with us. Can you imagine the fate of the prodigal son if his father had met him with veiled sarcasm instead of open arms?

Plan Your Liturgies

A well-planned liturgy is evidenced by the participation of lay women and men whenever possible. Prepared readers, music that is prayerful and relevant to the day's readings, and a homily that provides both insight and inspiration, all add up to an experience in community worship that will draw people back again. One would need little convincing that God is alive and well in such a parish. This is in stark contrast to churches that are cold, silent, and methodical in their worship. Some parishes seem closed, withdrawn, and uninviting, even to active members.

Good liturgical celebration is one of the Catholic church's greatest strengths; you do not need to have a full-time liturgist on your staff to ensure good liturgies. Books, articles, and programs directed toward building a strong liturgical community are available in every Catholic bookstore. While your local diocesan chancery can direct you to people who can help you get started, we have provided you with a list of helpful resources.[1]

Nurture Acceptance

Often overlooked by parish leadership is the fact that the word "family" no longer means the same thing to everyone sitting in the pews on Sunday morning. The old stereotypical Catholic family of mother, father and children in parochial school does not depict the way most of us now live our lives. Prayers, petitions, and ongoing church activities should reflect the recognition of singles, couples without children, the elderly, solo parents, families with children in public schools who care deeply about the spiritual formation of those children, and people living in and coming from dysfunctional families. The spoken word during liturgies and the messages in your parish bulletin all reveal whether or not your parish truly welcomes everyone. We hear too many sad stories from seekers whose feelings of isolation were reinforced by parish communities that still cater to an outmoded concept of the typical Catholic family. Perhaps your parish is open to everyone, but the message isn't getting out. Now is the time to explore ways to do that. It isn't enough to state that you are a welcoming parish; this has to be the actual experience of those who worship there.

One woman's journey of reconciliation began after a memorable Mother's Day on which she had forced herself to attend mass. Newly divorced, she was raising her children alone. She already felt the burden of guilt and limitation so common to single parents. Feeling totally abandoned by the suburban parish where she had been active all her life, she deliberately drove off to an unknown parish, far from her home that morning. There she was startled by a homily that focused on motherhood from the perspective of single mothers: their struggle and their contribution to the church and society. There were no negatives! Only support for a difficult job done well. The woman ended up joining that parish and eventually recommitting her life to active ministry in the church.

As church, we have to recognize that good people have human problems that need to be addressed in our communities. Divorce, death, chemical dependency, problems with children, mental and physical illness, abuse, and economic insecurity are only a few of the agonies common to human beings from all walks of life. Too often these situations invite condemnation and scorn from fellow parishioners, heaping even more grief and shame on those struggling with these heavy burdens. A parish atmosphere of self-righteousness and condemnation is likely to be created by people who dare not recognize their own problems, lest they too be judged. This is not an atmosphere that encourages honesty, growth, development, and maturation of faith.

Parents often come to our sessions looking for a place to talk about their adult children who have left the church. They feel too ashamed to discuss this with people in their own congregations. Their first question always is, "Where did we go wrong?" It is hard to grow through any experience if our whole focus is on where we went wrong and who will find out. As Christian community, we should encourage people to recognize and grow through these difficult spots in their faith journeys, promising them support and prayer through the whole process. Then we can truly celebrate and understand the victory of the risen Lord when we come together in the Eucharist.

Provide Education for the Entire Community

If your major parish focus is on its school and the families whose children attend it, people with other needs and gifts will not be drawn to your community. There should be well-prepared education programs for people of all ages, from all walks of life. Ongoing education is vital to those who are recommitting themselves to the church. Once committed to a journey of faith, most seekers are no longer content to sit passively in the pews; an honest faith search is never ending. Programs do not have to be elaborate or sophisticated. In fact small groups of faith sharing and Scripture study, or mini-series that explore topics that affect day-to-day lives may be more successful than expensive, high-powered programs that leave little room for human interaction and diversity. Whatever the program, it is essential that it be guided by sound, theological comprehension of church, its history, and its mission.

Develop a Reconciling Pastoral Staff

Before beginning any outreach to inactive Catholics, it is imperative that your pastor and pastoral staff are actively involved in the effort to welcome people to your church. Their role is vital in the development of a welcoming attitude among the community. There will be those who feel insecure or threatened by the idea of including *everyone* in your welcoming message. It takes sensitive, compassionate ministry to help these skeptical parishioners reach a point of such absolute acceptance. We must be careful that in our zeal to welcome some, we are not callously alienating others.

We urge people who are contemplating a ministry to inactive Catholics to contact their pastor and pastoral staff members for a very candid discussion about their own approach to people who are struggling with church and faith issues. Once during a meeting with the pastoral staff from a parish determined to begin such an outreach, we were stunned to hear the pastoral minister state defiantly, "These people need to accept the fact that the rules are good for them!" Another time we heard a pastor deny any need for listening or for free discussion, determining that all the seekers need is "more education." Still another parish priest insisted that there be no mention of the word "divorce" in any parish outreach activity. It is essential that the pastoral team present a unified concern for the seekers and a shared commitment to accepting people where they are.

The pastor and staff play another significant role in a reconciling parish. It is not enough for your parish bulletins, announcements, and your liturgies to indicate that this is a caring community of believers. That message must be backed up by acknowledging that your staff has time for seekers who need to draw on the community for support, comfort, and direction. These pastoral services should be easily accessible and available to everyone, regardless of membership. If your parish has these support services in place, people need to know that they exist and how to plug into them. We are saddened when seekers tell us of unmet needs that could have been met had they known of help that was available. In this era of enormous parishes, many who regularly attend mass have no idea of the pastoral services being offered. This information must permeate the entire congregation as well as the surrounding secular community. Parish members can serve as significant resource people if they know what your parish offers.

We are not suggesting that every parish must financially sustain a staff of paid pastoral ministers. That is usually impossible. But every parish can prepare committed lay people to assist in pastoral ministry. Often these are the very people who have already struggled with and survived the same kinds of hardships that will cause others to ask for their help and understanding. As they minister to one another, they acknowledge and give witness to a loving, forgiving God who will not only guide them through hardship but also make them stronger and wiser in the process.

Christians don't welcome struggle or enjoy it more than anyone else, but we do believe there will be new joy, new hope, and new strength at the end of our struggles. Also, from a Christian perspective, we often discover through hardship that our own giftedness becomes more apparent than before, when life seemed easy and predictable. Seekers welcome the kind of honesty that is evident in Catholics who acknowledge their own struggles; they can identify with the faith of those who go on, even though the answers are not always readily available. Seekers do not relate to Catholics who value obedience above all else and who question nothing. Most of us really don't feel like saints down deep inside and therefore we may prefer to worship with a community of acknowledged sinners!

Obviously not every parish will have the financial ability to provide programs that meet every need. That is why we think it may be time to look seriously at more interparish cooperation so that human and economic resources can be utilized more efficiently. Parishioners should be invited and encouraged to attend programs at other churches. As Catholics, our local parish experience sometimes belies the universal character of our faith. Instead of cooperation, we often pit one congregation against another. These attitudes of isolation and superiority do not present an inviting atmosphere to newcomers, and they impede the mission of the church.

Encourage Freedom to Choose

Forced attendance at a parish determined by geographic boundaries must not be a stipulation from a community embarking on a ministry to inactive Catholics. Fortunately many bishops have already removed this arbitrary means of assigning parish membership. As Catholics become more and more enlightened about their faith, its history, and its call to each of us through baptism, we are less willing to worship in a parish where we are neither nourished nor challenged spiritually. Essential to those reconciling with the church is a parish community that invites them to a particular sense of belonging and where their gifts are going to be welcomed and received. Choosing to belong to such a parish takes on a whole new meaning of being Catholic.

Practical Suggestions

Here are some practical suggestions you may want to try if you are committed to making your parish a welcoming community:

Greeters, Welcomers:

More and more parishes are calling forth ministers of hospitality, people who commit themselves to the crucial but simple task of welcoming everyone who enters the parish doors, especially during the weekend liturgies. It is not enough that ushers direct traffic from the church vestibule! This is an especially good ministry for those whose lives are already overcommitted; while they may not be able to attend evening meetings and programs, they can spend a few extra minutes each weekend simply being friendly to parishioners arriving for mass. This is a ministry that reaps instant gratification; it's fun to watch Catholics respond to a warm hello on their way into church.

Greeters can be of any age. Some parishes invite their young people to be greeters; others rely on senior citizens. Others rotate from Sunday to Sunday, allowing representatives from all parish organizations to serve. The only qualification required is that the greeter enjoys the job and wants to be there. This is not a ministry for the "drafted."

Ushers:

A short time ago, we visited a parish in a small rural community where the ushers greeted us with stony faces and silence. (We were surprised since we had been invited by a parish group that said they wanted to make their parish more welcoming.) During our talk, we suggested that ushers could serve as greeters in small parishes where there were more jobs than people. The pastor reported to us afterward that the ushers had stormed into his office after our visit and declared, "We are not going to be friendly!" The fact is, however, that in more and more parishes, ushering is a ministry of hospitality. For that reason, effort should be made to encourage ushers to understand the importance of their role in parish hospitality.

It is important to expand this ministry to include all members of the community. Some parishes commission families or married couples to usher on specific Sundays. It is a small step, but most women, children, and young adults express enthusiasm when they realize this ministry is now open to them.

Visitor/Parishioner Cards:

This is an excellent beginning project. Visitor cards can be placed in the pews or in the pamphlet racks at the entrance of the church (see Appendix, p. 202). The most effective cards are those that invite response not only from visitors but from parishioners as well. Many in your own congregation who would never have the courage to call the rectory will respond to this silent invitation to reach out for assistance. These cards are also used by people who volunteer to serve and participate in parish life. Visitor cards have a strong appeal for both active and inactive Catholics.

If you decide to use visitor cards, however, you must be prepared to respond to them immediately. It is best to contact every person who submits a card within a week, either by letter or phone call. If these cards are to be effective, this kind of follow-up is essential.

Welcoming New Members:

While participating in the financial support of one's parish is part of belonging to community, it shouldn't be the primary indication that one "belongs." There are many innovative ways to welcome new members. Larger parishes may host dinners for new members on a monthly or quarterly basis. Each new person is invited by a parishioner who acts as sponsor during the getting-acquainted period. Newcomers and sponsors share information about themselves and the parish. Some parishes invite their organization representatives to these dinners so the newcomers are made aware of the full spectrum of parish activities and services.

Another possibility is to involve the entire congregation in the process of welcoming new members. Each new member is given, along with their box of envelopes, a teddy bear! Parishioners are invited to donate these teddy bears. Don't be surprised if, in a very short time, a collection of warm, cuddly bears gives evidence to all that yours is a parish that cares.

Smaller parishes may choose to acknowledge new members during the Sunday liturgy. Some present flowers or other small gifts to the newcomers, symbolizing the community's welcoming spirit.

Parish Socials:

Parish functions should be first and foremost social functions, not money raisers. If Catholics are encouraged and invited to live out their baptismal call to witness to Christ, they will assume their proper responsibilities of stewardship with only gentle reminders and proper information. Then parish socials can be just that—opportunities for fellowship, getting to know one another, and for celebrating highlights of the community and its members. A major event could be an appreciation night, when the pastor and entire pastoral staff host and entertain the parishioners, celebrating the community's gifts to the staff during the preceding year. These fun-filled evenings could include singing, dancing, and skits, moments of grace when everyone gets to know each other better and to appreciate the gifts of all, whether they be ordained, religious, or lay people.

It would be unrealistic to expect every parish to drop its customary fund-raisers. Economically we know that is not plausible. What we deplore is the too frequent practice of holding "ghost" festivals which are not festivals at all but rather an excuse for another collection. These harried money-makers offer only pressure and obligation to participants. We invite you to reflect on your parish fund-raisers and social events in order to make them opportunities for Christian fellowship.

Welcome Home Events:

If your parish is already a welcoming community, you may want to sponsor a welcome home event, opening your doors to all. This is literally an "open house," where everyone is welcome. The entire parish needs to be involved in this in order for it to be effective. Volunteers can set up phone committees who will call everyone in the parish to tell them what is being planned, asking them to extend invitations to friends and neighbors.

Some volunteers can design a flyer to be mailed to every residence within your parish boundaries (see Appendix, pp. 203-4). Others can do the necessary folding, stamping, or stuffing. If your plans include a liturgy, it should be simple and inclusive, one in which all are free to participate. This will avoid the discomfort surrounding reception of the Eucharist for non-Catholics and inactive Catholics who attend.

A social time should follow the liturgy; this can be simple refreshments or a meal, depending on your parish and the number of visitors you anticipate. Arrangements should be made for newcomers to be acknowledged and greeted. This is a time for friendliness and hospitality, not a discussion of the issues that divide us. It is also a time to offer hope to any who indicate they are interested in reconciliation. It is helpful if you can invite them to something specific as a follow-up to your open house.

A possible follow-up activity is a church tour. A pamphlet describing the church building and furnishings, along with brief descriptions, would be helpful.[2] You may want to include a diagram of your church.

Forming an Outreach Team

If your parish is ready to begin a serious outreach to inactive Catholics, it will be necessary to form a nucleus of committed, faith-filled people who will work and pray together. The formation and ongoing development of this group, or team, is key to the success of your program. A careful balance must be maintained between the amount of effort devoted to the ministry itself and the selection, bonding, and spiritual nourishment of those who minister.

The invitation to learn more about forming a team should be a public one, extended through the usual parish communication channels, that is, bulletin announcements, mailings, and verbal announcements. It should be made clear, however, that there will be a process of selection in the formation of the actual team itself. Simply stated, some are suited for this type of ministry, some are not. There is great harm in allowing anyone and everyone to participate on these teams, both from the standpoint of the seekers as well as from the team's perspective. You may want to schedule an open, informational meeting simply to discuss the issue of inactive Catholics in your parish area. Those who attend will be likely candidates for team membership. In addition to such an open meeting, your pastor or pastoral minister may want to contact parishioners whom they feel would be good team members, personally inviting them to attend the meeting. Often those most qualified are unable to see their own giftedness until it is affirmed by someone else.

The same kind of open, honest sharing that you will offer to the seekers should be a part of your team's selection and preparation. Include prayerful liturgies in this selection process and time for all of you to gather socially. Through the sharing, praying together, and fellowship, some will determine for themselves that they would be more comfortable in another type of ministry. In other cases, the team itself may determine that a member may have difficulty functioning according to the group's common purpose. It is important that there be enough open, honest revelation in this phase of formation to allow such a gentle confrontation to take place. We cannot expect the seekers to be comfortable and open with us if we are unable to be equally open among ourselves. A deep level of trust among team members is a must.

As our own ministry developed, we discovered new areas of training that were especially helpful to us. We hired professionals to teach us techniques of good listening and pastoral care. It is vital that our involvement be limited to those areas and that everyone involved clearly understands the difference between pastoral care and counseling. Pastoral care includes listening, befriending, and providing resources. It implies the ability to discern when someone should be referred to a licensed therapist. It assumes confidentiality and a perception of boundaries for both the seeker and the minister. Pastoral care is not ongoing therapy, problem solving, or diagnosing. In no way do we suggest that team members should serve as long-term counselors or therapists for the seekers. Nor is the seeker's journey to be clouded with the minister's issues. It is not a vehicle through which the minister works out his or her own issues of alienation, family problems, chemical dependency, or codependency.

It is important that anyone working in this ministry should be free to make a solid commitment to the team for a particular period of time. Because of the training and continuing support needed by those who work in evangelization, there should be a sense of continuity and bonding between the members of your team. If your team is large enough, you won't all have to attend every series of sessions, but each series should be staffed by the same people from beginning to end. This allows the seekers to form friendships and develop trust in people they can feel free to call upon at any future point of their faith journeys.

Unless you are establishing a specific youth outreach, most of the seekers will probably be in their late twenties and older. (It is quite normal for young people of all denominations to distance themselves from their church for a while. There is a growing need for the church to address those issues of concern to young people.) Therefore your team should consist of men and women of all ages and should represent married, single, and divorced constituencies. Remember, your team will be a first encounter with church for the seekers. It is important that the team itself reflects differences in lived experience within the church.

Who Is Called?

Ordained Clergy

We recommend the participation on your team of an ordained priest. Most of the people who come to our sessions grew up in a church that was defined by its clergy and the hierarchy. For the seekers, therefore, it may be necessary to hear a priest say "It is" or "It isn't" so. For these same reasons, seekers often associate the pain and rejection they experienced from the church with a particular priest or even several priests. The presence of a priest who is willing to listen unconditionally is an impressive message in itself. Some seekers will be leery at first, not daring to say everything that is on their minds. Certainly it is a first-time experience for them to be invited to do so in the presence of a priest.

In retrospect seekers tell us that a priest's presence at the sharing sessions was their first indication that the church had changed and that, as a team, we were more interested in them than our own agendas. They also tell us how important it was for them that the priest did not wear his clerics or collar during those sessions. It was a visible indication to them that the priest was a person not unlike themselves, someone who would not use his position to control or judge them. We have yet to work with a group where at least one person doesn't ask the priest who is present whether or not he agrees with what the lay facilitator may be saying about church. Their comment is usually something like, "What she is saying makes sense, Father, but do *you* agree with it?" We were touched during one of our sessions where the attending priest was a retired pastor whom we had never met. He sat quietly until the inevitable question was posed to him. Then he spoke with the authority of one possessing a committed faith, Christlike love, and the wisdom of experience. He admitted to being part of a very controlling church in his younger years of priesthood. But he had experienced, along with the church, a process of conversion that was far more gentle and accepting than what he had experienced in his youth. Because of that conversion, he completely understood and accepted what was being said that evening by both the seekers and the facilitators. The young woman who sat next to him had not been in a Catholic church in years; she wept when he finished speaking and again at the end of our session when we gathered for prayer. She has been energetically working on her reconciliation journey ever since, frequently reminding us of her shock at the honesty that took place in the presence of a priest that first evening.

And, for those who choose to celebrate the Sacrament of Reconciliation, the anxiety about finding a compassionate priest is alleviated if they've already gotten to know the priest on the team. In fact, seekers often look forward to celebrating the sacrament with a priest they have come to know and trust.

Priests and lay team members who work in this ministry open themselves up to related areas of pastoral care with the seekers, including counseling, spiritual direction, and resource networking. Some Catholics still feel it is necessary to work through their issues with an ordained priest. (As Catholics become more comfortable with lay people embracing their baptismal call to minister, this need may change. We hope so.) While we are fully aware of the increasing demands being placed on the declining numbers of ordained priests, we still choose to emphasize the need for clergy involvement in this ministry. Priests who have invested time and energy in this work tell us the rewards far outnumber the sacrifices; some say it is a powerful validation of their priesthood. It is impossible to work so closely with people struggling through honest faith conversion without feeling new depths in our own faith experience, whether we are ordained or not. Minimally, a visible sanction or endorsement of this outreach by your pastor or a consulting priest is essential.

Wounded Healers

Called especially to this ministry are people who have acknowledged imperfection in their own lives. Note that we call these people "wounded healers"; they are not the "walking wounded." There is a vast difference between people who have survived and grown through hardship and grief and those who are painfully struggling to survive. We do no service to the seekers, nor to ourselves, when we try to minister to others while we are still feeling broken and uncertain about our own lives.

But how do we know when we have healed? We offer these basic questions to aid in the assessment of our own recovery:

1. Do we feel stronger for having lived through the experience (illness, divorce, death, job loss, chemical dependency, etc.), or do we still feel weak and vulnerable because of it?

2. Do we understand ourselves and God better because of our experience? Do we recognize new strengths and gifts in ourselves?

3. Do we no longer need to go over and over the details? (Remember, this is a *listening* ministry.)

4. Do we feel a renewed sense of joy and lightheartedness, a hopefulness that we can share with others, or have we become angry and embittered?

Wounded healers rarely fall into the trap of becoming "fixers" who simply take over and tell a seeker how to resolve his or her faith dilemma. Having learned firsthand the value of working through their own issues, wounded healers are more apt to see the merit of a seeker's search as well.

Committed Church Strugglers

People who have ongoing struggles with church themselves, yet can still see in it the Body of Christ, are invaluable team members. It is perhaps impossible for those who have never questioned their faith to relate to the questioning of the seekers. Some of our best team members are former seekers who easily relate to the new seekers' doubts, questions, and anger, but who now accept the fact that the church is a human institution, capable of human error. As we grow and learn to accept and forgive our own imperfections, we become more tolerant of the church's human weaknesses as well.

It is not likely that those who have given up on church, or who are embittered toward it, can help seekers move past their own anger. This is a ministry of reconciliation. Effective team members need to have come to grips with their differences with the church, to have put them into a perspective that allows their church commitment to grow, while still working for change where needed. This can be an awesome demand, and at times even the most committed team members may need to step away from the ministry in order to reassess their own experience of church. We serve best in this ministry when we truly believe the church is growing closer to its mission of representing Jesus Christ on this earth. We cannot offer to others a hope that we ourselves have lost.

Necessary Characteristics of Team Members

The following characteristics in your team members will provide a solid foundation from which your ministry can function:

Personal Relationship with Jesus

It is essential that all team members have a lived relationship with Jesus Christ and have built their faith experience upon that relationship. It is this relationship that sustains us in this ministry, and it is this relationship that speaks to the seekers at the very root of their faith journeys. While the church is the means of expressing and celebrating that faith relationship, the team member's faith rests in Jesus, not in the institutional church. Many of the seekers have acquired a personal awareness of Jesus during their time away from church. They need to discuss this part of their faith experience with Catholics who live out such a commitment within the church.

Understanding of Current Theology

Obviously not every team member will be steeped in theology. But team formation should include overview courses and discussions that allow for an understanding of Catholic doctrines and teachings. Especially vital is a clear understanding of Vatican II and how it has affected the church. Many seekers have had years of Catholic schooling, and in order to have credibility, the team must have some theological depth. If you have a priest, religious, or pastoral minister on your team, that person may serve as the resource person for these issues.

Knowledge of Church History

In these times of change, it is essential to understand the history of a changing church and its ability to adapt across time and geographic boundaries. The minister should be able to find hope in the confusion and open disagreement so prevalent in our church today, hope in a church that is alive and growing. A historical perspective allows one to ponder past church crises, the people who lived through them, and the church that emerged from them. It is helpful to understand, for instance, the history that surrounds papal infallibility, celibacy, the Reformation, and marriage laws in order to consider the human contribution to the evolution of these teachings and to distinguish church teachings from "God's Law." Team members need to acknowledge those parts of church history that have not been holy at all without feeling defensive or minimizing their existence.

Scripture

Team members should understand the manner in which the Bible is revered by the church. If you can clearly state and defend the church's position on the Bible, you will never have to indulge in debates with fundamentalists over the rigid meaning and intent of individual passages. Such discussions are fruitless and detract from the overall group dynamic. Since the sessions are conducted in a Catholic setting, we prefer to acknowledge that we do not use Scriptures in the literal way that fundamentalists (Catholic or Protestant) do. Team members should understand this difference without feeling compelled to apologize for it.

Miscellaneous Characteristics

Definitely not called to this ministry are those who measure one's goodness by absolute obedience to the church. It is impossible for the seekers to relate to someone who simply accepts everything on blind faith, questioning nothing. Most seekers are on an honest faith exploration; they cannot change what they believe simply by being told they are wrong.

Generally people who value introspection and ongoing personal growth are best suited for this work. We need to be comfortable enough with our own limitations to feel unthreatened by the seekers. When we find ourselves arguing and persuading, we are not really ministering. Convincing is done by the Spirit; our job is simply to facilitate the flow of information. If we feel responsible for whether or not it is accepted, we may be trying too hard to accomplish our own goals.

As a team, you will need to remind yourselves constantly that there are no success/failure records in this kind of ministry. The Spirit is responsible for any progress made by the seekers. This view will help you take less personally those who seem to reject everything and refuse to go on in their search. Remember: we never know where those people may be led once they leave.

Inviting people to share their faith journeys also invites them to share their pain, failures, and personal stories. This intimate sharing can be burdensome and, at times, almost overwhelming to the minister. Without a team closely bonded in prayer and friendship, you may find yourselves unable to process or let go of some of these experiences. This is a ministry that truly honors confidentiality. Team members need to know that within the team itself they can seek counsel and comfort in a prayerful, supportive encounter without jeopardizing the sacred space shared with the seekers. Burnout is common among those who do not have, or do not avail themselves of, this type of spiritual networking.

Getting the Word Out: Extending the Invitation

You can't get started in this ministry unless the seekers know you are serious about inviting them back. Surprisingly, this third, vital step is the easiest: extend invitations. We do that through media, parish bulletins, preaching, mailings, and personal invitations.

We do not, however, go door to door, nor do we advocate expending lots of team hours on parish census or related projects, as this often results in a high burnout rate. You have only to recall your own reactions the last time someone from another denomination knocked on your door to understand why such outreach projects are seldom long-lasting. We state, more in truth than jest, that we choose our method for three reasons: (1) we are lazy, (2) we are cowards, and (3) we found a more successful way!

Were we not convinced that the Spirit will bring to us those who are ready to embark on a faith journey, our ministry would not have endured beyond the first year. You cannot force people to subject themselves to spiritual introspection without this leading by the Spirit. It is an indication to us that we are doing the Lord's work and not our own busywork when we are energized and exhilarated by our efforts, rather than exhausted and embittered.

Media

If you are truly preparing to embark on this ministry, one phone call to your local paper will probably generate some kind of story or commentary. Local newspapers will usually do an in-depth story. It is news in the secular world when a Catholic church decides to become a welcoming community. Sadly enough, our public image isn't very good in this area, so the public is interested in what we are doing. Local newspaper stories have brought many people to our sessions; they have also identified the parishes in which we run this ministry as welcoming parishes. The residual effects of such publicity are lasting.

Our primary invitation to the sharing sessions is issued through the major metropolitan newspapers, where we purchase advertising space on the Saturday church pages (see Appendix, pp. 205–6). Most often it is the only invitation listed from a Catholic church, surrounded by dozens of invitations from Protestant churches. If you advertise this way, include phone numbers of people available to minister to those who respond. It is equally important that your parish receptionist and office personnel are fully informed of all details so that they can field inquiries in a professional manner. A person who has been away from the church for a time may be discouraged by a phone encounter with someone who knows nothing about the sessions and who offers no assistance.

We hear touching stories about the newspaper invitations or ads from our seekers; many carry that little ad in their wallets for months before finding the courage to contact us. As a parting gift, an elderly couple we worked with gave us our ads, yellowed and frayed, from two papers. Each of them had secretly cut out and tucked away the ad, not daring to confide in the other. Those ads were three years old when they finally called us. When we asked why they waited so long, their reply was, "You were our last hope; neither of us could face losing that hope."

Do not underestimate the impact of your invitation in any public medium. Have you ever ridden on public transportation where you have little to do but read the advertisements? We were amazed at the response to the invitation we placed on Boston subways! Remember: there are 15,000,000 inactive Catholics in the United States and each day many of them use public transportation, listen to the radio, or watch television. We encourage you to creatively use media to extend the invitation to seekers.

Parish Bulletins

We've received strong support and response from the pastors in the Archdiocese of St. Paul and Minneapolis, where our ministry began. Each time we schedule another series of sessions, we write to them requesting that they place our invitation in their parish bulletins. At every session are seekers who learned of our sessions through these bulletin announcements. They may have read it themselves when they attended mass. More often a Catholic friend, coworker, or neighbor, who thought they might be interested, has shared the bulletin announcement with them.

Preaching and Prayers

As discussed earlier in this chapter, your pastor's support is essential to any outreach in your parish. Some pastors devote homily space to this ministry; others write letters to their parishioners asking for their prayers and support. Every effort communicates your parish's concern for inactive Catholics to the community.

Informing Parishioners

Because we wanted our own parishioners to be involved and supportive of this outreach, we asked for volunteers who would phone every parish household. We wanted to inform all parishioners of our progress and to ask for their prayers for us and for the seekers who would respond to our invitation. Many senior citizens offered to shoulder this important task. This kind of grass-roots support should be developed and encouraged. Seekers may sit next to parishioners in the pews one day; it is important that the entire congregation be aware of the role each person can play in extending a warm invitation to seekers.

Mailings

We have also used parish mailings, again utilizing gifts and talents of parishioners in design, advertising, layout, and mail distribution. Low-cost bulk mailings are sent to every household within designated zip code areas. Our experience indicates it is better to send two or three mailings, stressing a similar theme and logo, at regular intervals than it is to put all your dollars into one high-cost mailing. If you use mailings, remember that the message has to be simple, nonthreatening, and inviting. Like the newspaper ads themselves, they serve only as gentle invitations.

Personal Invitations

Many inactive Catholics are simply waiting for an invitation to come to a session. Don't be afraid to extend a personal invitation. Sometimes we underestimate the effectiveness of a personal invitation extended by a trusted family member or friend. Give it a try; you may be surprised at the results.

No matter what form you use—newspaper ad, parish bulletin, homily, mailing, or personal invitation—be sure the invitation is gentle and appealing, without any demands on the seekers to phone ahead, make reservations, or pay fees. This is one parish outreach where we must not pass the collection plate!

And now, at last, you are ready to begin. Your parish has become a house of welcome and prayerful support for your outreach, you've formed a team that can pray and work together, and you've extended your invitation into the secular community. It's time to wait, pray, and trust the Spirit to carry that message to those who are looking for it.

Collaborative Outreach Ministries

It may not be possible, however, for your parish to accomplish the three major steps alone. If this is the case, consider networking and collaborating with other churches. There are sound reasons for such networking. Less than 1 percent of the seekers who have come to our sessions live within the boundaries of our parish. Many tell us they would not have responded to such an invitation in their local parishes, because they need anonymity.

Because of the investment of time and money required to train and prepare a team for this ministry, the advantages of drawing from a larger base are obvious. Most parishes are neither financially able, nor equipped with enough staff, to provide the needed formation and support for such a team. Because of the transient nature of our society, team members will leave and need to be replaced. Therefore if the ministry is to remain vital, ongoing recruitment and training of team members is necessary. This is the dilemma we face in our own small parish.

Our ministry has grown far beyond the parish's ability to sustain it. The financial burden of training team members and the necessary advertising for the ministry cannot be incorporated into the parish budget. Stipends we receive for presentations, seminars, and workshops on outreach to inactive Catholics are funneled back into our own parish program, but these outside activities draw enormous amounts of energy away from the ministry itself.

One alternative would be to have formed and sustained teams through diocesan offices of evangelization, and then assigned to deaneries, vicariates, or otherwise defined segments of local dioceses. Since we rely most heavily on advertising in the secular media, and since the seekers themselves prefer a program with less parish focus, it would be more cost effective to approach the ministry from an overall diocesan or regional perspective. Team members solicited from a deanery or vicariate could pool educational and personnel resources from their respective parishes. It doesn't seem prudent, or even desirable, for every parish to involve itself in a ministry that reaches beyond parish boundaries.

We have a few words of caution, however, about a diocesan program. This ministry must be approached from the seekers' point of view, not from the point of view of the professionals who may be sponsoring it. The value of teams composed of mostly laity is their constant day-to-day lived experience "in the trenches"—their jobs, their homes, and their churches. The laity's view is very different from that of chancery offices where programs are designed to meet timetables and departmental budgets.

We are continuously changing and adapting our format in response to the seekers' needs. That is how our program has evolved. We dislike programs based on quotas, set agendas, and expectations. The Holy Spirit doesn't have a lot of room to function under those conditions. We would not recommend embarking on a ministry such as this without acknowledging first and foremost that it will, in essence, be the Holy Spirit who does the work.

Of equal concern is the reality that seekers may not trust a program officially controlled and directed by the institutional church. We know of instances where empowered officials have negated the hard work of committed clergy and laity. After having begun programs on their own, they accepted backing from official church offices and then found themselves compromising the integrity of their programs because of conditions, totally unrelated to the seekers' needs, placed on them. It is easy to feel exploited under those circumstances.

We think a balance is possible. In most instances, we have received open support from bishops, education directors, offices of evangelization, and local clergy. We hope for increased dialogue and a heightened awareness of the need for all of us, as church, to commit ourselves to reaching out to our baptized brothers and sisters who want to resume practice of their faith. While we see great value in regional concepts of this ministry, we are fully aware that there are many parishes that are ready and eager to begin active ministry and evangelization efforts to inactive Catholics on their own. We encourage them to do so.

Chapter 4

THE MINISTRY:
Step-by-Step

In the previous chapter, we suggested the important preliminary concerns, including how to get the seekers to your sessions, that must be considered before you attempt our model of reconciliation ministry. In this chapter, we focus on what happens once the preparations are made, the invitations are issued, and the seekers respond.

The description that follows is based on several years of experience in the metropolitan areas of Minneapolis-St. Paul, Minnesota, and Boston, Massachusetts. Initially, we did not sit down and draw up an outline of this process; rather it has developed through prayerful discernment of our own experience and the needs of those who come to us seeking possible reconciliation.

To simplify the description of our ministry, we divided it into three parts: the initial session, the immediate follow-up sessions, and the ongoing contact with the seekers. Each part has a different purpose and dynamic. However, before looking at these parts, let's take a quick look at presession preparation.

Before the Initial Session

Decide when to hold your sessions based on your particular needs. We usually hold ours on weeknights, alternating the day of the week from one series to another to accommodate those who have standing commitments on particular evenings. Occasionally, if the need is indicated, we will hold sessions on Saturday afternoons for those who work evenings, or for the elderly or others who find it difficult to venture out at night. The time you select will depend on the makeup of your community. If your community includes large numbers of working parents evening sessions work out best. Our sessions last for one and one-half hours. You may want to meet for two hours, but we would not recommend longer than that, especially not on the first evening.

Prior to our initial session, ads appear in local newspapers for several weeks, inviting inactive Catholics to the meeting. Mailings have also been sent to area pastors, asking them to place similar invitations in their parish bulletins. Other flyers and announcements also have been used to publicize the meeting (see Appendix, pp. 202–4). You may find other ways to do this, including personal invitation and referral, but the important thing is to get the word out to inactive Catholics that these sessions will provide an opportunity to talk about why they are away from the church.

The specific team members who will host the series of three sessions should now be selected. We recommend that the team should never be larger than the group of seekers who attend the session. Since this number is an unknown, it is sometimes difficult to know just how many team members you will need. You may want to experiment with your own format in order to determine what is best for your parish or pastoral setting.

An ideal team for each series of sessions consists of one facilitator and two or three other team members. One of the team members should be a member of the clergy or a religious. This fulfills the seekers' common need to have an "official" church representative present during the discussion. It seems to give the meeting more of a sanctioned status for some, while others find that the presence of clergy or religious enables them to vent their frustration more freely.

The session will go more smoothly if you have an experienced facilitator on your team. The role of the facilitator at this first session is:

1. To continue the atmosphere of hospitality. Hospitality is a priority at this session. The facilitator has key responsibility for creating a welcoming and nonthreatening environment.
2. To enable group discussion. The facilitator must temper those who dominate the conversation and encourage those who may be quiet or too apprehensive to raise their issues.
3. To keep order. Creating an open atmosphere where seekers can share feelings about God and church can lead to volatile debates or arguments. The facilitator must keep order in a way that does not hinder the discussion.
4. To encourage seekers to share issues. With the assistance of a chalkboard or newsprint, the facilitator invites seekers to compile a list of topics for discussion.

We encourage the team to arrive at least forty-five minutes before the start of the session, as this allows adequate time for prayer. Prayer before and after each session is invaluable. When we join together in prayer, we empty ourselves of any expectations for the session. The nervousness and anxiety about how many people will participate or concern about the potential topics gradually gives way as we ask God's blessing on and guidance for the seekers and ourselves.

After prayer the team concentrates on hospitality. We cannot overemphasize the importance of a hospitable environment at this first session. Just as we would welcome seekers into our homes, we help them to be at ease in this, our spiritual home. This hospitality must begin the moment they enter the parking lot or the front door. Literally some of our team members serve as greeters in the parking lot in order to give a bit of welcoming encouragement to apprehensive seekers who might be confused about which door to enter. We try to alleviate every potential source of apprehension.

When the seekers enter the meeting room, they are welcomed by team members who offer coffee, tea, or a cold drink, along with assorted snacks. We have name tags available and invite everyone to use only their first names. Team members mingle with the early arrivals, helping them to feel comfortable. It is not at all unusual for seekers to arrive twenty or thirty minutes early. For many, the decision to attend has not been an easy one. It may be their first time in a Catholic church in many years, and the time spent waiting for the meeting to begin may seem like hours to them. The atmosphere of the entire evening is created during this waiting period. Casual conversation about the weather, the length of their drive, or how they heard about the meeting can help to initiate conversation and take some of the pressure off the seeker. It may help when you sense a fair amount of apprehension to reassure the seeker that these sessions have been going on for some time, and that the team members are all practicing Catholics. As angry as seekers may be about the church, most want reassurance that they have truly come to a place where they will meet people who can speak from a position of active church commitment.

Sitting in a circle works best for the sharing process. A circle defuses the classroom or lecture atmosphere of the session. Team members find it easier to disperse through the group and the circle encourages active listening and eye contact with the seekers. We never make the cirle too large. It is preferable to start off with only twelve chairs and then increase the number of chairs to accommodate seventeen people. If we begin with twenty chairs and only twelve people show up, the eight empty chairs can create an unneeded barrier between participants.

In the beginning, it will be normal for your team members to feel overwhelmed or apprehensive about the session. After all, many seekers come with great expectations. Some hope that their issues will be resolved after one session. While making our limitations clear to the seekers, it is also important for us as a team to recognize these limitations ourselves. We cannot be available to all people, all of the time. Neither can we solve all their problems. It is imperative that we continually remind ourselves and one another that we do not do any of this work without God's assistance. We rely on the power of the Holy Spirit.

Initial Session

PURPOSE: To acknowledge each seeker's presence within a group setting; to hear their stories; to validate their pain; to correct misinformation if needed; to offer opportunity for private discussion and fellowship.

MATERIALS: Chairs, sign-in sheet (optional), blackboard or newsprint pad, name tags, pens, chalk, markers, and refreshments.

We deliberately do not begin this session with prayer; it is important for the introduction to this process to be as non-threatening as possible for everyone who attends. Many of the seekers tell us that prayer at the beginning would have seemed like an imposition to them. Many feel compromised when they are forced into prayer situations while they are still harboring resentment, anger, and confusion about their church relationship. Prayer is seldom a fruitful experience without the presence of a strong element of trust—in God and among those who are praying. At the designated time, a team member officially welcomes the seekers who have gathered. In the opening remarks, the importance of confidentiality is stressed. We ask the seekers to respect one another's views and issues and to consider the evening as sacred space: whatever is said there will remain there. We promise not to reveal what individuals have said and we ask the same from the seekers.

To avoid anxiety we clearly state that the session will end in one and one-half hours and invite those who would like to meet individually with a team member to do so after that time. We announce that we will allow forty-five minutes for these one-to-one meetings, explaining that the team needs to excuse itself for prayer and processing after that time. If we are not clear about these time restraints, many seekers would continue discussing their issues for hours. As a team, we have always stressed the importance of keeping this ministry in perspective. We meet with the seekers for a designated period of time, but we must also have the opportunity as a team to minister to one another.

As a warm-up exercise, we give personal introductions, beginning with the facilitator and going around the circle. We simply ask the seekers to introduce themselves and tell us how they learned about our session. (Team members give their names and identify their participation as team members.) Some will only give first names; others feel free to give their full names. We ask how people learned about the session to help us determine where our advertising efforts have been most effective, which papers are bringing the most response, and which parishes are placing our invitations in their bulletins.

Next the facilitator invites the seekers to reflect on the statement, "The thing I DISLIKE most about the Catholic church is ..." We offer encouragement at this point since it is sometimes hard for the seekers to comprehend that we are actually inviting them to state openly their grievances with the church. It is important to begin with negative issues; after all, these issues brought them here and are why they are estranged from the church. We can't expect them to put those issues on hold while we present our own agenda. Trust begins to build the minute seekers realize we mean what our invitation said: we will listen to whatever they have to say, no matter how unpleasant. Frequently the invitation to list their dislikes is met with silence. You can feel the tension in the room as the seekers nervously look at one another, or stare at the floor. In retrospect they tell us that silence meant they still could not believe anyone representing the Catholic church would propose such an opportunity. If the silence persists, we gently nudge them by reminding them that they have come because of a concern or issue with church and that it is our hope that no one goes home without at least mentioning his or her issue.

It is important at this time for the facilitator to explain that the objective of the exercise is simply to compile a list of DISLIKES. The group is asked not to give a long explanation of their issues, nor to discuss the issues at this time. We urge them instead to express themselves in a few words or not more than a sentence.

One by one, issues are offered at random. We make no effort to go around the circle. This is not a time to force anyone into saying something. Once everyone has had the opportunity to share one issue, we invite additional responses. The list often gets very long and the seekers begin to interact with one another as they realize they are not alone in their particular feelings of anger or frustration. In order to prevent this process from turning into discussion, the facilitator may need to remind the group that discussion of the issues will come later once the list is completed.

When the list is finished, we offer the seekers an opportunity to generate a second list. This time we ask them to reflect on the statements, "The thing I LIKE most about the Catholic church is . . ." The process for this list is the same, but do not be surprised if you find that this list is much shorter!

This second list is used for several purposes. First, it points out very quickly that the LIKE and DISLIKE lists can overlap. This illustrates that the church, as well as those of us who are gathered at this meeting, is very diverse. We have many different spiritual needs and life experiences. We may like or dislike different aspects of the church, spirituality, and theology. This is why we request that discussions not deteriorate into judgments or discussion about various LIKES or DISLIKES. Rather, we encourage the seekers to listen, support, and try to understand one another. This point must be emphasized from the beginning; if not, a free-for-all is possible. Issues that appear most frequently on the two lists are:

DISLIKES	LIKES
Traditions	Social action
Statues, rosary	Stability
Repetitious prayers	Capacity for change
Infant baptism	Eucharist
Poor are ignored	Vatican II
Focus on money	Statues, rosary
Confession	Marriage preparation
Bingo	Sacredness of art and
Position on homosexuality	music
Position on masturbation	Appeals to logic
Position on premarital sex	Daily Eucharist
Too family oriented	Position on abortion
Impersonal	Mercy and forgiveness
Pope	Liturgy
Papal authority	Tradition
Celibacy	Pope John XXIII
Mary replaces God	Music
Guilt trips	Quality of higher edu-
Divorce, annulment	cation
Remarriage laws	Universal
Too much change	Hospitals, nursing homes,
Position on birth control	charities
Boring liturgies	
Exclusiveness	
Lack of Scripture	
Legalism	
Parochial schools	
Abortion	
Lack of emphasis on Holy Spirit	

The team's main function during this part of the session is to listen and observe, not to offer their own likes and dislikes. It is our task to assist the seekers as they work through their issues of alienation, not to work out our own. Once both lists have been compiled, the facilitator invites the seekers to begin discussion with any issue from the DISLIKE list. They are usually quicker to respond this time and the fun begins. Now the facilitator really begins to work. A good facilitator must remember not to let any one person or issue dominate the discussion. Everyone must be given an opportunity to speak freely about any issue that appears on the list. If one person seems to dominate, the conversation can be directed to another person by saying, "Let's give someone else who hasn't said anything so far a chance."

Sometimes a session can get off course. Any one of the many topics on the list could fill the entire ninety minutes. The facilitator must watch the clock and keep the conversation moving as much as possible. If much time has been spent on one topic, or if the discussion has moved off the designated issue, the facilitator may say, "I am aware of our time limits and the fact that we have a large list of issues to talk about; could we move on to another topic?" or "Perhaps you'd like to discuss that issue further with a team member after the meeting."

During this discussion period, the team can be supportive by offering appropriate information or affirmation. Gentle encouragement to continue, affirmation of the seekers' goodness, and validation of their hurt-filled experience can all help troubled seekers finish stories that are almost too painful to tell. While this support may include a team member acknowledging a similar feeling or experience, the focus remains on the seeker, not on the team member. The team's primary function is to *listen* to the seekers and to *observe* the process taking place.

If it becomes obvious that a seeker wants to learn more about the annulment process, for instance, a team member who has been through the process can offer to talk with that person afterward. Many issues can be discussed more freely and thoroughly during these valuable one-to-one encounters which follow the larger meeting.

Occasionally a seeker's pent-up anger or hurt seems to explode; it is as if once detonated, the blast cannot be stopped! It is important to allow that person to say and do whatever is necessary for them. Giving seekers space and permission to vent these feelings and frustration is an essential ingredient of this ministry. Do not be afraid when this happens. Do not try to prevent it, even if you and the group are feeling uneasy. This may be part of the bonding process for the entire group; the team and the other seekers know what is going on in the heart of the speaker. Many are able to personally identify with what is being said; it is touching to observe these strangers reaching out to one another with support and encouragement.

An appropriate response to an outburst, which may be anger, crying, or simply the revelation of raw pain is silence. It is a good time for silent prayer. After a moment or two, an apology, in the name of the church, can be extended. Some seekers appreciate a hug or some physical sign that you are available to them, even at this dark moment in their lives. Support and compassion from team members is a must. There is no one prescription for these occasions; as time goes on, you learn to trust your hearts for the proper response.

The facilitator may take this kind of outburst personally. Remember, neither the facilitator nor the team members are under attack; we cannot take responsibility for the seekers' pain. Good team processing following the session can be helpful in restoring everyone's perspective.

Another extremely difficult situation is an encounter with fundamentalist Christians. You can usually spot them right away. They come prepared, with their Bibles in hand. These individuals are rarely seekers. They usually come to accuse the church of its sins, to use their literal interpretation of Scriptures to make judgments, and to argue. They claim a priority on the possession of truth and often are not willing to join in open discussion.

This is not only frustrating for the facilitator, but it disrupts the group discussion and process. If you sense that this is happening, calmly and clearly ask these individuals to respect the process, which allows everyone an equal opportunity to speak. If they refuse to do that and continue in their judgmental attitude toward what the seekers are saying, we do not hesitate to ask them to leave. In front of the group, we extend an honest invitation to meet with them later when we will be happy to listen to them and their issues. We don't want to cause undue alarm, however. During the time that we have been hosting these sessions, we have only had to use this drastic measure twice. In neither case were we contacted for a private meeting.

"Traditional" Catholics in the midst of a more "progressive" group can also cause some uneasiness. Since most seekers are struggling to discover a more personal, less institutional experience of church, the more traditional seeker may feel out of place. In these situations, gentle reminders to the entire group will help preserve the atmosphere of respect for each other's issues. It always helps if the facilitator affirms the goodness in the seeker who is sharing, reminding the group to focus on the *person* and not the *issue*.

When the designated quitting time arrives, a team member thanks everyone for their participation. An invitation is extended to participate in weekend liturgies and to come back the next two weeks for follow-up sessions, which are open only to those who have attended this initial meeting. Allowing new people to join the group each week diminishes the group's ability to grow beyond the anger expressed during the first session. Expressing that anger is essential to the reconciliation journey and newcomers who haven't had that opportunity miss an essential part of the process. For these reasons, we never advertise the follow-up meetings in our initial ads. We tell seekers that the upcoming sessions will focus more specifically on Vatican II and changes in the church, as well as their individual faith journeys. We end the session by joining hands while we say the Lord's Prayer together.

This closing prayer has been a powerful experience for many. Regardless of the negative feelings and attitudes that may have been expressed during the evening, this coming together in prayer seems to symbolize for them an experience of full participation in Catholic community. They nod in agreement when we explain that gathered there, in the presence of God and one another, we have been church. It is usually a moving experience for team members as well.

Finally, we ask the seekers to complete an evaluation or information sheet before they leave (see Appendix, pp. 207–8). We stress that this is optional; there is no pressure to have everyone do so. The questionnaire asks for basic information regarding how the seeker learned about the session as well as about the church issues that cause the greatest tension. While the form includes space for name and address, it is clearly stated that these are optional.

Once the session ends, the team circulates throughout the group, thanking the seekers for coming, answering questions, offering resource referrals, and listening. Often a personal invitation to meet for Eucharist on Sunday is gratefully accepted. It is important to use this time to make personal contact with as many seekers as possible. It is here that real bonding occurs between the seekers and the team.

When the seekers have left, the team meets for what we call processing and shared prayer. This processing is an essential component of this ministry. These sessions can be very draining; we need each other's insights, support, and evaluations. This process time allows us to share our own observations concerning the session. Frequently a team member who sat across the room from a particular seeker can offer powerful insights because he or she could observe the seeker's facial and body expression while we, who were sitting next to the seeker, were limited mostly to hearing and peripheral vision. Others draw from their own experience in assessing a seeker's story and provide new dimensions of understanding for the entire team. It would be impossible for the facilitator, or any one team member, to absorb the full impact of all that goes on during these first sessions. Remember the importance of this process time for your team!

Finally, in prayer, we turn all the pain and hurt that has been shared that evening over to the Lord. We place the seekers' lives during the coming week in God's loving care, asking the Spirit to comfort and guide them. Without this prayer time it would be impossible for us to go home feeling at peace with God or the church.

Before leaving, the evaluation sheets should be distributed so that letters can be sent by team members to those who provided their names and addresses. The letter expresses our gratitude for their presence and participation and serves as a reminder for the two follow-up sessions. Team members should sign these letters and mail them the next day. The seekers' response to this follow-up has been very positive.

Follow-Up Sessions

PURPOSE: To provide additional opportunity for discussion of seekers' issues; to address most significant issues raised in DISLIKES list from Session 1; to explore seekers' concepts of God; to move seekers into general awareness of post-Vatican II concept of church and adult conscience formation; to allow seekers to interact with team members and one another, thus experiencing a new concept of church, one in which they are free to participate.

MATERIALS: Tables, chairs, pencils, appropriate worksheets, refreshments.

It is important that the first follow-up session occurs the week immediately following the initial session to preserve continuity and momentum. While we normally schedule two of these follow-up sessions, the number could be three, four, or five, depending on your own program. Some parishes have established programs lasting up to a year.

The format for the follow-up sessions is different from our first gathering. Since these gatherings are not open to newcomers, the bonding between seekers and the team which began during the first session goes uninterrupted. In the few instances when we have made exceptions, we have noted an obvious impact on the group dynamic. If clearly explained, the seekers understand why their friends, or a family member, or someone at work cannot join them for the rest of the series. They understand the value of that first session's experience in their own journeys. Many will ask when the next series is scheduled, or whether someone they know can meet with a team member in the interim. We try to accommodate these requests as much as possible.

Numbers are smaller for these meetings. While many accept the invitation to air their issues during that first session, fewer are willing to make further commitment to any reconciliation process. This can be discouraging if you are just beginning this ministry. If thirty-five people attend the first session and only twelve return, there is a tendency to ask, "What went wrong?" But experience has taught us that few inactive Catholics are interested in devoting the time and energy required to a genuine reconciliation journey. Those who find our ads or hear about our program may come to one meeting out of simple curiosity. Some see it as an opportunity to restate their position about the errors of the church but have no interest in looking deeper into the church and into their lives. Others are simply not ready to embrace the process yet, but they may be in two or three months—or even a year. Remember: numbers in this ministry are not important. What matters is helping those who *are* ready through a process of reconciliation. The follow-up sessions are much more personal, with the focus on each participant's faith journey; therefore you will find the smaller numbers a distinct advantage.

At these sessions, we sit around a table or group of tables, depending on the size of the group. This seems to better connect the seekers and allows those who want to take notes or complete the worksheets that we use to do so. You may prefer to continue in a circle setting; feel free to adapt to your own circumstances.

We begin these sessions with an appropriate prayer or Scripture passage. We prefer extemporaneous prayer, with references to pertinent events of the day, which may include the weather, news events, and our shared journeys of reconciliation. While placing our gathering clearly in God's care, we acknowledge ourselves as people connected to one another by our common daily experience.

We sometimes use the daily Scripture readings, stressing the common bond that takes place throughout the world as these same readings are reflected upon wherever mass is said that day. Or we will select a reading that emphasizes God's love, forgiveness, and healing. Sometimes we choose a psalm that expresses the same aching longing for God that the seekers expressed during that first session. The passage you select should reflect your journey thus far with this group of seekers. It should uplift, encourage, and assure the seekers of God's unconditional love.

Following this opening prayer experience, we give the seekers an opportunity to address any unfinished issues from the week before. Their responses can contribute to the agenda for this meeting, especially if they reveal a need for clarification or explanation. Do not be surprised, however, if much of the anger has been muted during this week. Often the group, strangers one week ago, seems to have bonded to one another and is eager to move on.

It is important to allow the seekers time to reflect on the first session's impact on their lives, as well as to process what they've experienced since that session. Many are astounded by the effect that session has had on them throughout the week and welcome the invitation to discuss that with one another.

The focus during these sessions is moving the seeker beyond the pain and anger surrounding specific issues. We are not suggesting that you try to avoid either the pain or the issues. But by now, most seekers who are exploring reconciliation find it more helpful if the conversation is directed toward fruitful and life-giving topics such as God and Jesus, especially as they relate to their own lives. A sensitive balance must be maintained between the need to pursue painful issues and the effort to move forward in presenting positive realities of our God and our faith.

Helpful Topics for Follow-up Sessions

- The reality of God's love and whether or not we are able to translate that love into self-love. This includes our image of God, how it was formed, by whose influence, whether that image has changed over the years, and how we communicate with God (prayer).
- Spiritual conversion as an ongoing aspect of life versus a one-time experience, or obedience to rules.
- How religion has changed, Catholic and Protestant; effects of culture on religious experience; Vatican II changes in light of the history of change in the church; sacraments — what are they and what is their role in the life of a Catholic? Different ways of celebrating Eucharist and confession.
- Adult conscience formation; results of faith based on obedience; assuming responsibility for our own relationship with God and church.
- Exploring aspects of change in our lives and how that has affected our relationship with God, our understanding of who God is, what church is.
- Values: What are our own? What are the church's? How do they relate to church teaching? What are society's values?

Good facilitating skills are required for this process. An intuitive sense of what subjects to cover results from a prayerful consciousness of the needs of each particular group of seekers. Therefore the subjects vary from series to series, session to session. This is not a "one-size-fits-all" ministry! A helpful resource in opening an informal but very personal discussion about God, faith, and religion is *How to Reach Out to Inactive Catholics.*[1]

Any discussion that narrows the seekers' focus to their own self-images and God's unconditional love for them will initiate this process of spiritual self-awareness. We often begin by asking, "If Jesus is truly the Son of God — a God who loves us — and if Jesus was truly sent to die for our sins and provide everlasting life for us, why is only 25 percent of the world Christian?" This usually leads to a discussion about how we as Christians and as church measure up when it comes to simply loving one another. Then the discussion goes on to Jesus' commandment "to love God with one's heart, soul, and mind — and to love our neighbors *as ourselves.*" While the conversation usually probes what it means to love others, to be loved by God, and to love within a community, invariably it leads to a discussion of whether or not we are capable of loving God or others if we do not first love ourselves.

The outer discomfort of the first evening frequently moves inward now as the seekers discover their difficulty in comprehending a God of love or in talking abut themselves in a loving way. Many have been taught a piety in which sainthood is achieved through self-degradation or denial. To speak of their human existence in terms of being lovable, good people is pathetically difficult for most.

Since we learn about God from others, we explore the role of parents, teachers, and friends in formation of the God concept. Again the discussion usually comes back to self-image and reveals tragic concepts of God imparted by key individuals in the lives of the seekers, as childhood memories are probed and shared. This discussion may become extremely poignant.

Worksheets stimulate discussions about God, faith, prayer, and religion (see Appendix, pp. 209–11). But any resource material that enables the seekers to reflect on topics of deeply personal significance is helpful. Not only do the worksheets bring feelings and thoughts into focus, but those feelings and thoughts become less threatening to share with a group once they've been written down on paper. Even those seekers who are not ready to reveal what they have written find the reflection itself to be therapeutic and healing. Some quietly tuck the worksheets away in order to devote more time to them in the quiet of their homes.

Helpful in our discussions of ongoing conversion is a chart like the one on p. 109 that clearly illustrates the process of conversion. It allows the seeker to let go of the idea that individual acts or deeds determine one's relationship with God or the church.

Essential to the reconciliation process is a setting that invites and encourages open sharing among the participants. Free-flowing conversation about seekers' self-images, families, and relationships with God becomes the catalyst to self-discovery and often reveals the root cause of alienation from the church. For most people this journey of reconciliation is a time of deep growth spiritually and includes other aspects of their lives, because of the time and space this process allows for introspection. When the seeker can finally trust enough to allow God to enter into the painful memories and experiences in their lives, healing begins. These groups become beautiful examples of church as the team and seekers affirm, encourage, and accept one another in the process of self-revelation. A prayerful, sacred intimacy develops that is a gift in itself to those who gather.

Discussing Values and Change

Seekers seem to appreciate a discussion of values and the opportunity it provides them to reflect on their own values as they relate to church and society. Most observe that this is the first time in their adult lives that they have devoted time or discussion to something that lies at the core of their being. The chart on p. 110 offers a helpful comparison of ancient Catholic values and values associated with today's American individualism.

The Process of Conversion

Type	From	To
AFFECTUAL	Blockage of feelings	Acceptance and ability to use feelings
INTELLECTUAL	Knowledge as facts	Knowledge as meaning
MORAL	Satisfaction or law as criteria of choices	Values as criteria of choices
RELIGIOUS	Life as series of problems: "one damn thing after another..."	Life as mystery and gift

Specified in:

THEISTIC	God is a force	Personal relationship with God
CHRISTIAN	Historical Jesus	God's love for me in Living Risen Christ
ECCLESIAL	Church as "THEY"/ an institution	Church as "WE"/ a community

SOURCE: From James Dunning, *New Wine, New Wineskins* (Chicago: Sadier, 1981), p. 23.

In discussing change and its presence in church, we also point out that discontent has always been a part of church experience. Seekers are often surprised to hear that ours is not the first generation of disgruntled Catholics! We consider Joan of Arc or St. Francis of Assisi as people who challenged acceptable church lifestyles and doctrines. The church becomes more relevant to seekers as they contemplate the role of prophets in the church and consider who today's prophets might be who are

Differing Views of the Human Person

Catholic Christian	*American Individualism*
We find wholeness in our relationships with others	Self is autonomous—totally independent of others
Natural, assumed interdependence within society	Social ties result only from free contract between autonomous beings
Moral coresponsibility for human dignity, suffering, freedom, etc.	Naturally and morally independent of one another
Center of value: God and others	Center of value: Self as individual
Values derived from relationship with God and others	Moral values reflect private taste
Private moral values affect our choices and actions in public/work sector.	Private moral values apply to home only. Marketplace is for pursuit of self-interest.

SOURCE: Adapted from Robert Bellah, et al., *Habits of the Heart* (New York: Harper & Row, 1985).

calling the church to purify itself. Pope John XXIII, in opening the Vatican II Council, "called for a study and exposition of doctrine that would employ the literary forms of modern thought" and stated that "the substance of the ancient doctrine is one thing and the way in which it is presented is another."[2] Modern theologians such as Rahner, Schillebeeckx, Küng, Reuther, Boff, and Whitehead challenge all of us to examine ancient teachings in light of history's gift to us: a new understanding of reality. It is only through this ongoing scrutiny that our faith remains alive, relevant, and truthful. The seekers discover dignity in their own questioning once they realize that Catholic history is filled with faithful men and women, some now regarded as saints and some whose names we will never know, who questioned and challenged church teachings. They did not dissent because they desired to undermine the church or its authority, but because they believed sincerely that God was calling them to a different understanding of truth. Now aware that dissension from within has historically resulted in positive consequences for the church, the seekers are free to contemplate constructive ways in which they can effect change.

Change also involves the Protestant Reformation and how it changed the church. Because the church was confronted with radical opposition, its authorities seemed to rally the troops and circle the wagons in order to protect and preserve everything it held sacred. Any form of questioning or suggestion of reform was looked upon with suspicion. Those in authority were fearful of change. The seekers understand the human tendency to react defensively when we are challenged. The Counter-Reformation was clearly a defensive reaction as well. For the first time, the church hierarchy succinctly defined the meaning and number of sacraments, determined how and where weddings were to be conducted, declared marriage between a Catholic and Protestant invalid, and created the Index of Forbidden Books. A strict discipline was established and imposed on those wanting to enter the clergy. In short, the church's imposition of a rigid faith expression resulted more from its opposition to Protestant reforms than from revelation found in Scripture or tradition.

In light of their own human experience, the seekers begin to identify and understand the very human reaction of the church during the post-Reformation period as well as the lasting effects of that reaction. Many see a similarity today in the church's response to their own situations. Some of the issues that cause the most pain occur because of the church's inability to deal with dissension or change. Rather than talk about conflict or explore ways in which it could change, the church has a long history of simply avoiding it. This kind of discussion does not change the reality of church history nor the pain it evokes. It does provide some rational understanding through which the seekers can begin to assume personal responsibility for reconciling their inability to submit in blind obedience to any and all teachings of the church.

The seekers love to talk about Pope John XXIII and his vision for a renewed church. Most know very little about the effect Vatican II has had on the church, other than the obvious external practices. We speak of Vatican II as John XXIII's invitation for radical evaluation and reformation of the church; the seekers recognize the power of the Holy Spirit to bring change in spite of a church that resists it.

Exploring Personal Renewal

Moving from changes within the church to change that is necessary for personal renewal opens the discussion to how we are affected by change and whether we welcome it in any form in our lives. As we ask the church to be open to change, so we too must be willing to incorporate renewal into our own lives. The process of reconciliation demands that one be willing to consider changing old ways of thinking. Throughout the Scriptures, Jesus shares a message of conversion. In these sessions, we try to share with seekers a new way of experiencing God and church. If they truly seek unity with the Catholic community, the call to the table is one they have a right to choose freely, whether to accept or decline. As the Vatican II "Declaration on Religious Liberty" (#3) states: "the practice of religion of its very nature consists primarily of those voluntary and free internal acts by which a person directs one's self to God."[3]

Renewal means that the seekers are no longer children. Instead they are adult Catholics. It is their responsibility, with God's assistance, to decide what is right and wrong for them. We refuse to make their choices for them. Rather, we assist them in a process that will help them to gain those faculties required in order to make adult choices.

Development of a mature conscience is an important topic in this discussion about personal renewal. With simplicity and sensitivity, we help the seekers see the difference between an adult, fully-developed conscience and one formed as children by rules of obedience. Giving adults the permission to make choices is a new concept for the seekers. Making mature choices requires dedication, reflection, a sense of the sacredness of others, openness to church teachings, prayer, and Scripture. This new way of thinking usually cannot be absorbed in one evening. It becomes clear, however, that we are not talking about "doing your own thing."

A good basis for this discussion is the Vatican II "Pastoral Constitution on the Church in the Modern World" (#16):

In the depths of one's conscience, one detects a law which he/she does not impose on self, but which holds that person to obedience. Always summoning to love good and avoid evil, the voice of conscience can when necessary, speak to one's heart more specifically: "do this, shun that." To obey it is the very dignity of humanity, according to it one will be judged.[4]

The seekers can readily see that their childhood lists of rights and wrongs have not equipped them with the ability to make adult faith choices. This presents an opportunity to point out the truth that lies in the "heart of hearts" and the need to allow for the time and space to find that truth, to understand the whisperings of the Spirit. For some that will mean a painful journey, but it will result in a renewed experience of God and church.

Other questions that help focus these discussions on the possibility of renewal are questions like: What's the bottom line—what really makes us Catholic or Christian? Will that definition ever change? What happens if we stop changing or if the church stops changing? Will we no longer have the Eucharist if there aren't enough ordained men to consecrate it? These conversations help the seekers to fathom themselves as a part of change, rather than victims of it. Obviously we can't offer easy solutions, and the seekers know that. Our faith, like theirs, is also a journey and we invite them to journey along with us.

By the end of the third session, the group has become community to one another. Much of the anger has dissipated and a conversion of faith has begun to take place. We celebrate this new closeness in a short liturgy that acknowledges God's love for us and acknowledges one another for our gifts to the larger church community. If a priest is a part of the team, this liturgy can be the healing Sacrament of Anointing. In this prayer experience, we openly acknowledge our respect for the seekers who are at different points of their journeys. This becomes a soothing, gentle gift to those who have felt so disconnected from their church. But this acknowledgment does not mean that the healing or the journey has ended. It is not a closure to their faith journey but rather the beginning of a long process of prayer, spiritual discernment and, for some, reconciliation with the church.

Throughout these sessions, we continue to acknowledge God's presence in the lives of the seekers, regardless of their church relationship. We assure them that salvation is not contingent upon their church membership, but we offer the Catholic church as a way to celebrate their Christianity. By this time, through private conversations and group discussion, the seekers are aware that we as team also have our struggles with church and that in spite of those struggles, we see hope and promise in living out our lives as Catholics. If this message of celebrating one's Christianity as a Catholic is woven throughout the process in a gentle, positive way, seekers are more receptive to the possibility of affiliation. But our priority is not to "make them Catholic"; our purpose is to listen and assist in the healing process. When and if they are ready to talk about affiliation, we are ready to embark on that phase of journey with them. In no way is this ministry devoted to "sign on the dotted line and return to

Catholicism." It is committed solely to fostering the process of reconciliation for those who freely choose to participate.

We assist in that process of reconciliation when we talk about faith as movement or journey toward God's truth. To move toward that truth requires personal growth and acceptance. Our role is to affirm seekers' questions, to help them sort out doubts and accept their anger. We validate these issues because they characterize the seekers' individual faith experiences. For the first time, they begin to see that their faith is not weak but very much alive, even though painful.

We also talk about anger and how paralyzing it can be, and about its capacity to prevent growth in any relationship. We suggest gently that while anger may be directed at the church, some of it legitimately may be focused on those cultural or familial influences that have become enmeshed in our church relationship. We let them know that sometimes anger at church is an indication of unresolved anger in other aspects of their lives. Issues surrounding religion and family go hand in hand; and sometimes they become so entwined that it is difficult to sort out the complicated causes and effects.

As the sessions unfold, we may be alerted to those who could benefit from either spiritual direction or therapeutic counseling. If, after meeting with seekers in a group process and in one-to-one sessions, we see no evidence of healing or movement beyond initial issues, we encourage them to seek professional assistance. Therefore it is important for you to have a list of counselors, therapists, and spiritual directors for referrals. Especially valuable are Christian therapists who will respect and understand the seeker's desire for reconciliation with the church.

Ongoing Contact

PURPOSE: To allow seekers to continue their journey of reconciliation, offering opportunity for more formal instruction and individual guidance where requested.

NEEDS: Established agenda or curriculum. (This is most effective when seekers have presented items and issues to be covered. Provide ongoing opportunities for fellowship and community building. Provide resources for those seekers who are ready to reach out into other areas of church experience, such as liturgies, classes, sacramental celebrations.)

By the end of the third session, it is important to schedule individual conversations with those who are most eager to continue the process. Some may be ready to reconcile and will appreciate help in preparing for the Sacrament of Reconciliation. Others may need spiritual direction or further discussion about issues or topics that require more attention. Nearly all who complete these three sessions thirst for more; therefore we refer them to Bible studies, Catholic inquiry classes, or other adult education programs. Ongoing contact with a team member during this time is vital. The sense of community that was established in three sessions must be available for seekers who see that link as their only one with the mainstream church.

ReCollection: Delving Deeper

When additional followup discussions are necessary, a series of meetings called ReCollection is offered. ReCollection attempts to continue the process of reconciliation by gathering team members and seekers together for further reflection on their faith journeys.

ReCollection differs from the other sessions in that each meeting uses Scripture as a focus for group prayer and discussion. The topics discussed include alienation, reconciliation, Eucharist, and community. Each participant is given his or her own Bible. In the beginning of each session, we invite seekers to spend time in quiet and shared reflection on a specific passage.

If our topic is reconciliation, the group will spend the first part of the meeting praying over and sharing reflections on the adulterous woman, John 8:1–13. The remainder of the meeting focuses on our experiences of reconciliation. We also share contemporary theology and practice regarding the Sacrament of Reconciliation.

ReCollection is offered during Advent and Lent each year. Seekers tell us that those two times of year, significant Christian and family holidays, seem to be the most difficult periods during their estrangement from the church. ReCollection offers them an opportunity to reconnect. For many, it is the final step before reconciliation.

Many of the seekers who attend ReCollection welcome the opportunity to celebrate the Sacrament of Reconciliation. We respect the sensitivity of most who prefer not to do this in a public ceremony. Some resist being public out of a sense of shame, but most choose not to participate in any public acknowledgment of their status as inactive or alienated Catholics.

Wherever we conduct our sessions, we encourage those who return to active church participation to maintain contact with team members. They know we are available to them at any point of their reconciliation journeys. The seekers you met in Chapter 2 are still a part of our lives; for that, we are grateful. Margaret returned to her home parish, but we still hear from her through the thoughtful cards and letters she sends. We also see her at occasional workshops and retreat weekends. She calls seasonally for the Sacrament of Reconciliation.

Ann, on the other hand, became involved with the young adult ministry in our parish. She met new friends and pursues an interest in Scripture and theology at a local Catholic college. Our frequent conversations are important to her ongoing reconciliation process.

Ed lives in another city, but we still connect by phone calls now and then. He has enriched our life with his new insights and shared faith experiences.

Al and Ruth have become sacrament to us; these God-filled people witness to their new faith community as they cope with illness and the relinquishment of independence that comes with their advanced ages. They call for prayers now and then, and we are blessed by the assurance of their prayers for us.

Rick joined the parish and is facilitating a Scripture group for college students. Recently he enrolled in a Catholic college where he is pursuing a degree in law. His Catholic identity is strong now, and he is assuming an active role in a church that is eager to recognize his gifts.

It is important to remember that people like Scott, however, are not ready to reconcile with the church; they may never be. But the lines of communication are still open, and Scott knows that if and when he is ready to reconnect, we will be there. His faith journey continues and he has found spiritual peace. While his name may never appear in the reconciled statistics, his honesty and friendship and our respect for one another have made the process worthwhile.

Chapter 5

THE ISSUES:
What Separates Us?

As we have mentioned several times in preceding chapters, ours is a listening ministry. Our primary role is not to be preachers or teachers, but pastoral ministers. It is not to restate ancient theologies and rules, nor to present a God who cannot accept imperfection and variance in the human condition. Some may interpret our stance as one of leniency and weakness. We have discovered, to the contrary, that it is a powerful, effective approach in helping others find God's love. The gospel message is the foundation of all that we do. It is the core of our hope that we, as church, can be more loving, more accepting, and more nourishing to those who seek to know and respond to their baptismal call, to grow in relationship to God and to one another.

We see conversion as a multifaceted process that is neither completed nor defined in one lifetime. It is our job to help the seekers see the active role of God in their lives, rather than honing their awareness of human failure and futility. Without denying the presence of sin, we reinforce the sacredness of each individual and call forth that goodness within the context of Christian community, where we strive to live and to serve as Jesus did.

For several centuries, up to and including the middle of the twentieth century, pastoral care consisted mostly of diagnosing sinfulness, specifying degrees of severity based on the deeds of the sinners. Ordained ministers of the church prepared for their priesthood by diligently studying copious manuals that meted out prescribed punishments for specific sins. The rigidity of the manuals evolved from ancient teachings influenced by Aristotle, Aquinas, and Augustine. Assuming the role of spiritual parent, the church seemed to define God in terms of judge and controller of individual deeds and actions. Morality was defined objectively, with a resulting implication that "God said it was so." In practice, religion became separated from lived experience and the church became a place where the powerful (those who were ordained to judge) ruled the powerless (the laity).

Vatican II changed the concept of moral theology drastically and, with it, our concept of church. No longer called to a primary focus on sin, moral theology was to focus on charity.[1] From a pastoral perspective, the shift switched from law enforcer to compassionate befriender. The goal of the pastoral minister is to awaken the seeker to his or her own goodness, thereby empowering the call to participation in the Body of Christ. The pastoral minister begins, not with the law of God or of the church, but with the lived reality of the seeker. The more we can know about that reality, the more we can do to awaken the awareness of God in the lives of those to whom we minister.

No longer do we separate one's religious existence from the world itself. In its document "On the Apostolate of the Laity" (November 18, 1965), Vatican II recommends increased research and study, "not only in theology, but also in anthropology, psychology, sociology, and methodology . . . for the better development of the natural capacities of the laity—men and women, young persons and adults."

It is in the context of this spectrum of life that we reach out to the inactive Catholics. This is not a process of bringing back the lost, nor saving the unsaved. It is a mutual journey of conversion for the seeker and for the minister. It is a call to fullness and wholeness of life for both.

As we discuss the issues presented by the seekers and our response to them in this context, it is evident that your team must have depth and breadth enough for this pastoral approach. Again and again, you who minister will be called to reflect further on your own lived experience, to challenge your own truths. The task is not as simple as repeating rules and dogmas, nor defending the "system." This is not a ministry for those who value rigid certitude in their lives.

We have selected those issues that seem most common among inactive Catholics. We will present the seekers' perspective, the church's perspective, and the pastoral perspective. You will note the gap between these perceptions on some of these issues. The painful reality of this ministry lies in the fact that the church's official stance is often what Bishop Kenneth Untener of Saginaw, Michigan, referred to as "corporate severity." The bishop qualified his concerns by stating, "I believe that church ministers, when dealing one-to-one with people, generally tend to be very compassionate." In his address to the Michigan Religious Education Leadership Conference in Grand Rapids, Michigan, Bishop Untener said it is his dream that one day "because of our religious formation, we will stand out in the world because of our mercy as clearly as the Amish stand out because of their horse and buggy." Let us remember this shared dream as we explore the issues that challenge the Body of Christ's capacity to be merciful, for it is in the lived experience of the seeker that these issues of our faith have become stumbling blocks.

Hierarchy, Rome, The Pope

The Seekers' Perspective

- "The church is the pope and all those in power in Rome. They control our lives with little understanding of day-to-day problems faced by Catholics."
- "Church authorities misuse their power; this is offensive and irrelevant to modern life."

- "As Catholics, we have no say in our own moral guidelines, canon law, dogma, the papal letters. All are issued without consultation or concern. Our opinions, our life experience are of no value to church leaders. They have no appreciation for our faith experience at all."

- "We want more than hard rules and powerful leaders who discern God's will for us. We want to participate in the life of the church. We want leaders who care enough to listen to us, who communicate openly with us. We're tired of one-way communication from Rome which seems more intent on preserving institutional traditions than trusting the Holy Spirit to lead us to a healthier direction for the future."

- "We have lost hope in our church leaders. It is hard to trust and respect authority figures that neither exemplify nor draw on the true gospel message of service to one another."

- "As long as the hierarchy continues to cause pain for some, seems disinterested in what others are saying, and appears to be disenfranchising those who challenge their teachings, I cannot actively be a part of the Catholic church."

- "Whatever happened to compassion and understanding? I find more of that in other Christian denominations."

- "I'm tired of all these middle men between me and God. I prefer a personal, biblical Christianity without all the structure and outside authority telling me what I have to believe and do to be saved."

Church's Perspective

To help initiate a process of reconciliation in the midst of all this pain, hurt, and anger, it is important that the facilitator of these sessions convey as clearly as possible the basis of church teaching on this subject:

1. The church is not a democratic institution, but rather a hierarchical one; its organizational structure includes the

papacy at the top, with its ultimate authority, and individual members who are at the bottom with very little institutional or decision-making authority.

2. There is a difference between papal infallibility and the hierarchy of truths. Some church teachings are of greater significance than others.

3. Vatican II defines the church as the Body of Christ, composed of many parts, with each individual part vital to the whole.

Pastoral Perspective

That the church is not a democratic institution may be the most common complaint brought to our sessions by the seekers. It is helpful to point out to them that, as Americans, we tend to see all institutions from the unique perspective of our concept of democracy. We elect our leaders and indirectly have influence on what laws are enacted. If we are not satisfied with a leader, we can decide not to vote for that leader again or even to impeach him or her. And although minimally, our vote does affect which laws are enacted.

Because seekers have these same expectations when it comes to the hierarchy of the church, we have to be honest with them about the differences. The church structure is not based on democracy. One of the difficulties experienced by an ancient church is the baggage it carries from centuries of formation. Our hierarchical model of church is part of the legacy imposed on us by history. While acceptable and familiar to Catholics in the past, today's American Catholic expects to find a democratic process in the Catholic church. While we may share with the seekers our own desire for a democratic institutional church, we also help them see that such a change will be long in coming. When it does, it will be because Catholics have changed the way they experience their faith, not because the hierarchy will propose some new organizational flow chart. The challenge to us as Catholics, then, is to assume our sacred membership as equals in the Body of Christ. As the laity moves away from its spectator stance toward full participation and contribution, the church itself will reflect that change, regardless of its structure.

When responding to the issue of authority, it is also helpful to differentiate between pastoral letters and dogmas, and how they are connected with papal infallibility. Most seekers consider all documents that emanate from Rome to be infallible statements. It is important to clarify this misconception. When we explain, however, that pastoral letters are simply theological reflections on issues of pastoral concern for the church, many seekers become confused. They are not aware that these documents are an attempt to raise discussion and reflection on an issue, to explain the theology surrounding the issue, and then to propose a response to that issue. Few regard pastoral letters as an opportunity to inform, encourage, and support faithful Catholics, and most seekers are surprised to learn the purpose of these documents.

Because the contents of these letters are open to discussion and theological development, each pastoral letter is not infallible. An infallible statement is one that can never be open to change or theological exploration. Most seekers are relieved when they discover that very few statements from Rome are permanent, binding, and never open to change.

We explain a dogma as a doctrine that is promulgated with the highest authority and solemnity. When we say that Jesus is the Son of God, we are professing a dogma. Not to agree with a dogma is to question the very essence of our faith. Specific dogmas are not always easily recognized because they are such an integral part of our religion. A pastoral letter does not always imply that the issue being addressed is of highest authority or solemnity.

Pastoral letters and dogmas are distinct from papal infallibility, which is the pope's ability to make pronouncements on doctrines of faith that are "immune from error." Seekers, like most Catholics, tend to assume that anything and everything the pope says is final, binding, and infallible. It is important to correct that misconception and to point out that papal infallibility resulted from Vatican I, during which the Council Fathers declared that the pope could speak infallibly regarding matters of faith and morals. That occurred less than a century ago and therefore has been a part of Catholic tradition for a comparatively short period of time. This privilege has only been exercised twice, both times defining issues regarding Mary—her Immaculate Conception and her Assumption. These aspects of Mary's life had been a part of oral church history for centuries, however. The infallible declarations were set in a context of accepted belief and mythology, not from a startling revelation of truth experienced only by the pope. The important point to bring out for the seekers is that infallibility is not the personal prerogative of the pope. It is helpful to define the parameters of papal infallibility which pertain only to faith and morals, and include full participation by the entire College of Cardinals. Through discussion of these facts, seekers discover that this issue really isn't as significant as they were taught to believe. The pope simply will not wake up one morning and begin speaking infallibly about issues that will change our lives.

It may also be helpful to explain the teaching role of Catholic bishops. As teachers, they offer moral guidelines and focus attention on issues that can be helpful for us to examine in light of our faith in Jesus. We emphasize the values underlying the various controversial teachings and invite discussion on those values. The American bishops' statements on nuclear weapons and the economy are positive aspects of authority addressing issues of significance. The process by which these documents were written—open meetings across the United States, input from clergy and laity, several drafts and revisions—is one that is open and consultative and that includes input from Catholics of varying theological and political perspectives. Many times seekers find themselves in complete accord with the root values of these statements, thus enabling them to see their differences with church teaching as one of degrees, rather than total disagreement.

For those who have not actively participated in a church community since Vatican II, the concept of church as "they" is especially real. Authority was in the hands of the pope, cardinals, and bishops. It was natural for someone in conflict with the rules to feel resentment toward that structure. Vatican II however, changed that concept, emphasizing instead the church as Body of Christ. The accurate implication is that the church is much more than those who exercise authority. As the Body of Christ, church is composed of many parts, and everyone, regardless of their role in the church, is an important part of the Body. The Body will never reach completion until all its parts are able to work and pray together. Therefore church authorities without the laity comprise an incomplete Body.

We tell the seekers that as we gather together to discuss these issues, we are church. For many, this is the first time they have been an active part of church. Such an inclusive concept is new to them, and many cannot comprehend the full meaning at once. But, as it evolves, it allows them to appreciate the importance of their participation in a church that needs all of its members in order to be whole. It is far more comfortable for them to contemplate belonging to a church that values its individual members, than one that demands blind obedience to its hierarchy.

As resentment gives way to an appreciation for this new, inclusive concept of church, it becomes possible for the seekers to cite advantages in a church structure that allows it to transcend time, geographical, and political boundaries.

Preaching

Seekers' Perspective

- "Homilies, or sermons, are long and boring, irrelevant to my life."
- "I'm tired of hearing priests rant and rave about paying off the debt for the new church, social hall, or rectory."
- "I have to go to a Protestant church in order to hear a homily about Jesus and the gospel message."
- "Just once, I wish Father would include his own experience, questions and all, in his homilies. It would be easier to relate to what he says."
- "I need to hear more about my daily struggles as a Christian, things that I can use in raising my family, earning a living, relating to other people."
- "Why doesn't the priest ever explain some of these new church teachings to us, or discuss issues regarding sexuality?"
- "Please, can't we hear more about God's love and compassion, the gift of Christ's redemption for all of us, and less about God's wrath and judgment!"

Church's Perspective

Especially since Vatican II, great emphasis has been placed on the preparation of the homily. It is to be rooted in the Scripture readings for that day and have application to the daily experience of being a Catholic Christian. Homilies should offer encouragement and insights that will help the gathered community through another week of living out their Christian experience in the world. Actually, this is exactly the kind of homily most seekers are looking for. Oratorical eloquence is not nearly as important as a genuine message that connects the gospel, the priest, and the community with reality.

Pastoral Perspective

Our response to the seekers' criticism of homilies is agreement with their observations. We acknowledge the lack of consistency between their concept of a homily and that of the post–Vatican II church. It is painfully true that the experience falls short of the expectation. According to a 1988 Gallup poll, 21 percent of those who leave the church cite poor preaching as a reason. They are not alone; large numbers of active Catholics complain about this same issue. Poor preaching is a serious problem for the church; the content and length of homilies have become a common source of criticism and discontent. In many parishes, the time reserved for Scripture reflection has become something similar to a community bulletin board. Some priests use the homily time to address personal issues, parish finances, or other nonscriptural agenda. Others may reflect on the week's Scriptures, but their preparation is poor and their delivery is boring. Many priests are so pressed for time that they find it impossible to deliver new and refreshing homilies. Others simply try to "wing it" every Sunday.

While allowing the seekers to discuss these issues openly and honestly, we do point out the church's concern and its recent attempts to correct this problem. We tell them that workshops and training days that specifically focus on preaching, developing new preaching style, interpreting Scripture, and sharing one's personal faith story are available for priests in most dioceses. Also, seminary preparation now includes courses on effective preaching, both style and content. The church has placed a renewed emphasis on preaching the word of God. Announcements, parish concerns, or discussion of finances are more appropriately placed at the end of the mass.

Catholics who complain about poor preaching have a right to expect more and we make that right known to them. We do not hesitate to encourage seekers to seek out priests and parish communities that place a high priority on preaching and giving witness to the spoken word. After all, it is what the church wants for all of us.

Education

Seekers' Perspective

- "The God I learned about in Catholic schools was not a loving God!"
- "The nuns never encouraged us to question anything; anything they couldn't explain was a 'mystery' and we just accepted that."
- "We learned bigotry in the Catholic schools; there was one way to get to heaven and that was the Catholic way."
- "I can't imagine letting someone hit my children, but our parents never said anything when the nuns hit us."
- "Why all that money to educate children? What about adults?"
- "Our parish was nothing more than a school with a mass schedule; if you weren't involved with the school, you were an outsider."
- "Jesus was a historical figure who suffered because we were bad. I felt a lot of guilt about what happened to him!"

Church's Perspective

Historically the church school played a vital role in preserving religious and cultural identity for immigrant Catholics who came to this country. Often poor and lacking social and financial position, European Catholics found comfort in the structure of their local parish communities. As taught in many of those schools, religion did not contribute toward a healthy understanding of one's own faith or relationship with God, and certainly not an appreciation for individual differences and knowledge of other denominations and cultures. But the Catholic church was not alone in fostering this separateness. It surprises seekers to learn that Protestants of the same era were just as intent in maintaining their separate superiority. Culturally it was not a time for introspection or mutual respect within the American Christian church. But Catholics seem to bear deeper scars from that era; the vast school system allowed Catholic children to be shut off from the rest of society.

We are convinced that many of the issues and concerns that separate Catholics from their church are nothing more than childhood misconceptions of the Catholic faith. Yet until recently, the church made only feeble attempts toward educating its adults. It was as if a Catholic grade school or even high school religious education was sufficient to sustain Catholics for the rest of their lives. Consequently, as adults, many seekers feel inadequate and immature when it comes to understanding their faith and their church.

While the number of Catholic schools is declining drastically, the church is beginning to consider education in terms of a Christian's lifetime, rather than an isolated school experience. More and more parishes are opting for quality religious education programs for everyone, rather than a parochial school for a few. Many of the parochial schools that exist today provide an invaluable apostolate to surrounding neighborhoods by opening their doors to all children, regardless of race, nationality, or religious background. As such, they become powerful witnesses for the Kingdom, a place where children are accepted, nourished, and loved.

Pastoral Perspective

For Catholics who grew up in America, the school experience is the major common denominator. The sameness of the stories, regardless of who is telling them or where the teller grew

up, has been a revelation to us. One seeker can begin an anec-
dote only to have another seeker finish it out of an entirely
different church/school background. While the discussion
usually begins with humor, with one Catholic school story top-
ping another, it becomes more personal and often extremely
poignant as the session continues. On a general level, Catholic
parochial schools produced several generations of Catholics
who never doubted or questioned their faith as they grew up.
They were loyal and they were obedient. On a personal level,
these schools seem to have produced several generations of
human beings who come to us with feelings of guilt, shame, and
low self-esteem, all connected to their Catholic identity. This is
a lot of inner conflict to carry around throughout a lifetime, especially when learned lessons no longer apply to one's life or circumstances. With no real vehicle within the church to process
all of that confusion, many simply leave and decide not to deal
with it at all. While this is not intended as an indictment of
parochial schools per se, we have to validate for the seekers the
wrong that was done to them in so many of their school experiences, while holding out the hope that what was a typical school
experience in the past is no longer being perpetuated by the
church school system.

It is important that these stories are allowed to be told. Some
are amusing. Others are gruesome—like the story told by the
man in his forties who recalls with dread the time he was locked
in a closet for forgetting to wear his uniform belt. He was eight
years old at the time and still has difficulty talking about what
turned out to be one of the most traumatic episodes of his life.
It seems the Sister forgot that he was in the closet when she left
school for the day and the quaking, sobbing child was rescued
by a janitor who came in to do the floors late that evening.
While these stories are shocking in themselves, what is more
shocking to us is that no one remembers their parents objecting
to this kind of abuse. We encourage the seekers to talk about

today's heightened awareness of child abuse, an awareness that seems to have been nonexistent in previous generations, at least when these kinds of discipline were being meted out by the church.

The value in allowing the stories to be told, especially the deep, painful memories of childhood, again lies in the reexamination of those incidents from an adult viewpoint. Through this process, not only do seekers have the opportunity to vocalize their pain and see injustices for what they were; they also have their painful experiences validated by those present. We, as team members, facilitators, and ministers, often ask for forgiveness on behalf of the church for what amounted to emotional and psychological abuse for some Catholic children. Healing can begin to take place when such painful experiences are brought into the open and acknowledged, but the healing takes time.

Ironically, many of these same people who complain of excessive amounts of education and control during their childhood beg for more education from the church now that they are adults. Once they acknowledge that most of their church experience took place before they were old enough to comprehend either themselves or the world around them, a new curiosity develops. They want to know about the why's of what they were taught and how that teaching fits into the broad picture of church and American experience. They want a fresh look at Bible stories, with a more developed Scripture scholarship. Before recommitting themselves to the church, most seekers want to understand how it got where it is today and contemplate where it may be headed.

In essence, they want to use their newly discovered freedom to explore their Catholic identity as adults and to learn and grow in their awareness of all that implies. Seekers at this point of journey have crossed a major hurdle; directing them to appropriate church education programs may be all the further motivation they need.

Community and Parish Life

Seekers' Perspective

- "I don't feel like I belong, even though I've gone to the same church my whole life."
- "I tried to go back to church after being away for a while, but I felt so isolated and lonely there. There was no connection to anyone."
- "Catholic churches are cold, lifeless, and uncaring. How can I belong to a community that does such a poor job of reflecting Christ's love?"
- "The typical Catholic parishes with thousands of members and only one or two priests are just too big. There is no personal recognition, no contact with the priest."
- "Father looks so burned out that I don't feel like bothering him with my troubles. But who does a Catholic turn to when she has troubles?"
- "My parish favors those families that have been there a long time, those neat little two-parent families with kids in the parish school. There isn't anything going on for single people, those who are widowed, young adults, or solo parents."
- "I joined a Protestant church where I felt welcome. People greeted me at the door, introduced themselves to me, invited me to join in the life of the community right away. I didn't know such a thing existed in church until I became a Protestant."

Church's Perspective

In the past, Catholics belonged to the parish defined by the geographic area in which they lived or by the nationality of its members. That usually meant a church close to home and included the Catholic school where most of the neighborhood Catholic children were educated. The same people came and went to mass and the sacraments, but may not have developed close, personal ties with one another—even over a span of generations. Families watched other families grow up, knowing little about them or their private worlds of sorrow and joy, success and failure. Those things stayed in the family; they did not belong in church. Worship was an especially private matter; a very pious person attended daily mass, various novenas, benedictions, and other church devotions. Whether or not he or she participated in the social life of the parish or neighborhood was not important. Church was there for the dispensation of sacraments and salvation. Vatican II, however, brought new life and meaning to the concept of Catholic community life, although the meaning of the word community may be lost for most Catholics who have been away from the church for a long time. For those who grew up in the pre-Vatican II church, community referred to religious orders, where priests, brothers, or sisters lived and prayed together.

It is a paradox that at this point in history the Catholic church is made up of enormous congregations and at the same time, we Catholics are learning what Christian community in the early church was all about. The challenge faced by the post-Vatican II church is whether or not one can truly experience Christian community in sprawling parishes that provide weekend liturgies for thousands.

Pastoral Perspective

For those who tell us they dislike the cold, disconnected environment of the Catholic church, we may need to describe this new awareness of church as community and the efforts being made within the church to achieve it. It is reassuring for seekers to know that their desire for a church home where they cannot only give and do for others, but where they can also be nourished, challenged, and reconciled is a desire shared by most Catholics in the post-Vatican II church.

We can offer hope to these seekers because we see an ongoing effort by both clergy and laity to foster such a spirit of community and belonging, even in the largest of parishes. Clusters of small groups that offer opportunities to share one another's faith experiences, support for those who need it, and genuine Christian fellowship are becoming more and more the norm in Catholic parish life. As lay ministry becomes more defined and developed, we are convinced we will see even more of this kind of ministering to one another within the larger parish structure.

Community also brings new dimensions to the way we celebrate the sacraments in the church these days. No longer individual ceremonies where we were instantly infused with a special measure of God's grace, sacraments are now seen as celebrations involving the entire community; they acknowledge the recipient's new role in the community and the community's promise to foster and encourage the individual.

The relational aspect of all of us as Christ's Body and Blood, not just members of the local parish, brings new power and vitality to the Eucharist and its call to each of us to live out that witness to the entire community. It is also the basis for our longing for the return of these seekers who no longer participate in that sacrament: our community wholeness is lessened by their absence.

Expressed in the light of Christian community and the powerful, symbolic message they bring to us, the sacraments become for the seeker a reassurance of their union with the whole church. Through baptism, they too were called to community and the ongoing discovery that it entails. It is a welcome experience to see this awareness permeate a mind previously convinced that the sacraments were merely constant reminders of their separateness.

However, as we point out over and over in this book, what may be a hoped-for ideal for one group of seekers can be a threatening obstacle for others. There are those who complain that they don't like all of this new friendliness in church. The sign of peace is a weekly source of anger and resentment for many raised during a time when church was a private matter and you didn't get involved with your neighbor. It is sometimes tempting to become impatient or judgmental with folks who seem so unwilling to open their hearts to one another.

Instead we try, through gentle listening and affirming, to build a trust level with them so that a flow of give and take can begin to take place. Only then can they start to relax and respond to the group's acceptance of them. Often such a closed attitude is based on a feeling of discomfort, inferiority, or total bewilderment about what their church is asking of them. It is exciting to see people who are great-grandparents opening up and risking deeper involvement in their churches and with one another.

For most, community is a positive experience, and our message to those seekers who have not found it in their local parish is very definite: find a parish community that not only meets your needs but also one in which you can participate, share your gifts, and grow. Given an opportunity to discuss this, the solution usually becomes obvious. Seekers can hardly blame the church for all of their Sunday-morning anxiety when they haven't even tried to find a different parish community.

Some find Sunday mornings themselves a drudgery because of their unresolved issues with the church. We suggest they give themselves a break and try a new parish every now and then, perhaps meeting a friend for mass in a different parish, followed by brunch where they can talk about the experience. Once the pattern of "mass as a drudgery" is broken, seekers feel free to worship honestly in a parish community that moves them along on their journeys of faith. They also begin to see church in a new light. For so many, the only church they know is the one they were exposed to during childhood, or the one in the neighborhood where they now live. It becomes too easy then to discard the entire church if that immediate parish experience has been a consistently negative one.

As much as we dislike using them, the labels "conservative" and "liberal" are a part of church jargon these days. Once such a label is embraced by a particular parish community, it may exclude all those who do not identify themselves as such. Rather than hanging in and fighting for acceptance, we again suggest that seekers find a community where they can worship in comfort.

This is a caution to all of us who remain in the church—to reflect on the kind of image presented by our parish communities. If only one extreme of theology is experienced by a congregation, that parish is really not presenting an open message of Christ's love to everyone. We need to make room in all of our parishes for all people, regardless of where they are in their faith journeys. We give especially strong encouragement to seekers who are ready to reconcile with the church to find a parish community where they can participate fully, where they can share their gifts with the entire church. It is exciting for those who have been inactive for a long time to contemplate such a feeling of belonging. Because of the honesty and prayerfulness of their faith journeys, most of these reconciling seekers are no longer content to simply sit in the pews on Sunday. Blessed are the communities that embrace them!

Jesus

Seekers' Perspective

- "Not until I became a Protestant did I understand what it meant to center my faith on Jesus."
- "The Catholic church doesn't understand, nor share with its members, what it means to have a personal relationship with Jesus Christ. I recall only rarely hearing Jesus mentioned at all in the church where I grew up."
- "All those years in Catholic schools and I had to go to another church to learn the essence of being Christian; I feel cheated, robbed, that I wasted so much of my life trying to obey man-made rules in order to be saved."

- "We heard a lot about Mary, the saints, the rosary, all kinds of devotional practices. Where was my friend Jesus in all of that?"

- "In the Protestant church where I worshiped, people openly talked about their relationship with Jesus. They weren't ashamed to share their faith experience with me. They introduced me to Jesus through the gospels. It has changed my life."

- "I would come back to the Catholic church if I knew I could continue to grow in my personal relationship with Jesus there. Is it possible?"

- "I've given up looking for Jesus in the Catholic church. I have become a _____ [Protestant denomination]."

Church's Perspective

Perhaps the seekers who are most surprised by our sessions are those who have left the church because their Catholic experience focused so little on Jesus. Because the commonality between those who root their faith in Jesus Christ is readily apparent, these seekers soon discover that our sessions are conducted in an environment of faith that is deeply influenced by Jesus. As one young man put it, "I was shocked to hear Catholics on the team talk about their own personal faith in Jesus; I didn't think Catholics ever did that." Except for those who have been deeply entrenched in fundamentalist concepts of Bible study, these seekers, bonded in Jesus, may be the easiest to help move through the reconciliation process. Many have been away from the church for a long time and are totally unaware of the changes that have occurred during their absence. The current emphasis on Bible scholarship, personal Christian commitment, and empowerment of baptized laity are all marvels they had no idea coexisted with being Catholic. Most in this group have already grown enough in their faith journeys to have overcome the obstacles of guilt and excessive obedience, the two traits most common to many seekers. But those seekers who have committed to lives centered on Jesus Christ too often assume they cannot celebrate this faith in the Catholic church.

Pastoral Perspective

As facilitators of this process, we can validate the new awareness of Jesus developed by seekers during their time away from the church. It is helpful to explore various theological concepts of Jesus that encourage deepened understanding and reflection of who Jesus is, what his mission was, and what that mission asks of us. For those whose concept of Jesus was defined by a fundamentalist faith experience, the Catholic perspective of considering Jesus in the context of a broad spectrum of historical and theological truths can bring new life, excitement, and challenge to Christians. Two helpful resources are *Models of Jesus* by John F. O'Grady and *Jesus in Focus: A Life in Its Setting* by Gerald S. Sloyan.[2] Frequently such new perspectives enable them to discover a heightened meaning and sense of belonging in a church that is increasing its focus on the significance of Jesus in the journey of faith.

Divorce, Annulment, and Remarriage

Seekers' Perspective

- "My kids don't want me to get an annulment because it will make them bastards."
- "Why should I pay blackmail in order to get a 'Catholic divorce'?"
- "Frank Sinatra [or some other famous person] got an annulment because he knew the right people."
- "I know someone who paid $2,000 so Father would get them a 'quickie' annulment."

- "I won't get an annulment because I don't want to fight with my 'ex' again. The civil divorce was bad enough; I just couldn't go through it again."
- "My divorce wasn't a sin; it was the only healthy alternative I had. I don't need that piece of paper to know I'm okay with God!"
- "I've never been married or divorced, but my Protestant fiancé was. Now the church says *he* has to have an annulment in order to marry me in *my* church!"
- "How can a celibate priesthood dictate rules that govern married relationships?"
- "What does a celibate know about the devastation that comes with a broken relationship, or an abusive one?"
- "My kids' lives are ruined because Father wouldn't give me permission to divorce."
- "I was a lector in my church, the parish where I had lived all my life. When my marriage ended, Father told me I couldn't lector anymore. He even asked me to quit the choir."
- "How can this be allowed in a church which is supposed to present Christ's forgiveness to all? Why, in the entire realm of human failure, is this one area allowed to remain outside the redemptive power of Jesus?"
- "What right did the church have to give my partner an annulment, to say we weren't married, when I say we were?"

Church's Perspective

A good deal of misinformation about church teaching has to be clarified on these issues before any attempt can be made to reconcile with the church. The Council of Baltimore in 1843 did place excommunication upon divorce, but forty-one years later, seeing that this was far too severe, the Third Plenary Council of Baltimore of 1884 withdrew the censure.[3] The removal of this censure is one of the church's best-kept secrets! It is another false assumption that divorced Catholics who remarry are excommunicated; that excommunication was rescinded by the American bishops in 1977. The late Father James Young, C.S.P., clarified the relationship of remarried Catholics to the church: "Catholics who marry a second time without the church's approval are told that they're excommunicated. Nothing could be further from the truth. No matter what happens to the marriage of two Catholics, no matter how many times they get divorced or remarried, they remain Catholics."[4]

The church teaches that marriage is a sacrament, a covenant that cannot be broken. Implied in that teaching is that those who have divorced and remarried, without annulment, are unworthy of receiving the Eucharist. The phrase once used was "living in sin," and remarried Catholics are painfully aware that the label is still part of Catholic vocabularies. Too often divorced and remarried Catholics have been told only the stern reality of their legal status. They are unaware of the church's emphasis on compassion and understanding toward those in difficulty. In 1981 Pope John Paul II stated, "I earnestly call upon pastors and the whole community of the faithful to help the divorced, and with solicitous care to make sure that they do not consider themselves as separated from the church, for as baptized persons, they can, and indeed must, share in her life. . . . Let the church pray for them, encourage them and show herself a merciful mother, and thus sustain them in faith and hope."[5]

Pastoral Perspective

While categorizing the topics of divorce, annulment, and remarriage together, we need to see them as individual dilemmas in the lives of many Catholics. Each carries its significant amount of pain, isolation, anger, and shame. Lumped together in the life of one individual, the feelings are so many, so varied, and so painful that it becomes a major challenge just to sort them out.

Usually, however, the three words spill out of a seeker's mouth in one breath at those first sharing sessions. Quickly heads nod in support of the brave soul who had the courage to speak the words out loud in a Catholic setting. While some are able to express deep anger at the church's insensitivity to their pain, more often we see quiet tears, eyes void of hope, resignation to a life of banishment. These are the people who profess deep longing for the sacraments, for belonging to a church community, for participation in liturgies. These are often people whose brokenness has made them aware of a deep spirituality, one which is neither acknowledged nor welcomed in the Catholic church. When we began this ministry, our initial response to seekers who came to us with these issues was one of deep sorrow and frustration. Their pain was so evident, as was their goodness and often their patience with a church that had rebuffed them so blatantly. Words seemed totally inappropriate and inadequate in light of the shattered lives unfolded before us. From those on our team who had experienced divorce, we learned of the tremendous grief, guilt, and loneliness that accompanied that experience, along with an almost intolerable sense of shame and failure. Many of these feelings are too painful for the seeker to express; it is the minister who must acknowledge and thereby give permission for the pain to be verbalized.

We have learned since those early days, however, of the powerful energy and spiritual strength that lies beneath the woundedness of so many of these people. That knowledge has fortified our ministry and given us great hope, not only for the seekers but also for the church, which will be blessed by the very gifts made present through that woundedness.

We begin by acknowledging that hope, by asking forgiveness for the pain heaped upon them by the church's insensitivity to their grief. This honest exchange needs to take place before the onset of any instructional activity.

Rather than offering a series of legal loopholes and methods that will reconnect them to church, we prefer to start with an understanding of what a sacramental marriage is. In follow-up groups where the issues of divorce, annulment, and remarriage are prevalent, we provide information about the meaning of the sacrament before inviting the seekers to discuss issues surrounding marriage. Presenting sacrament as the community's recognition or celebration of an event that has already occurred, and acknowledging the ongoing connection of the recipient, the community, and God that is brought forth in that celebration, presents a strikingly different concept of marriage than the old stereotype of sacramental marriage. Marriage is not a one-time "zapping" at the altar! It is an ongoing communion between two people and their God, always growing closer in their relationship to one another and in their response to the community around them. It is a union characterized by cherishment, from God and one another, a cherishment that fortifies and nurtures the couple's call to reach out to others, first within the family, and then beyond. This is the marriage that is likened to Jesus' love for his church, a far cry from the "Offer up, put up, and shut up" attitude pathetically prevalent in some Christian marriages today.

In this new understanding of sacramental marriage, the seekers can finally begin to assess that prior bond for what it really was; this new perspective helps them to forgive themselves and their former partners for failing in that marriage. But it gives them something more: an excitement and expectation for what Christian marriage can and should be. It is in this excitement that we see healing begin and new horizons of hope open up for the seekers. In claiming their brokenness and in understanding what sacramental marriage truly is, many of them begin to live out lives that stir up within the church a renewed sense of what marriage is. Perhaps more than in any other area of our ministry, we see the resurrection most clearly in the lives of this group of wounded people who experience not only healing and reconciliation but even a call to serve the brokenness of others.

Paulist Father James Young provides hope for divorced Catholics with these words:

The spirituality, the holiness, that we see emerging among separated, divorced, and remarried Catholics in the United States is . . . a spirituality, a holiness born of suffering, rejection, and pain, rooted in the real struggles of everyday life, yet reaching to God and finding him coming to new life through that very suffering and those very struggles. Spirituality and holiness in the Christian community takes on many authentic shapes and styles, but the earthy style of the divorced is one the church needs today.[6]

Can you imagine the impact on someone who has felt estranged and shut out by the church for years when they hear these words? Very recently at a Second Marriage Retreat at Christ the King Retreat Center in Buffalo, Minnesota, Father Bill Fournier, O.M.I., welcomed participants and assured them of their rightful place within the church by virtue of their baptism, emphasizing, "We, as church, *need* you." That is a far cry from being tolerated or endured in some kind of back-pew membership. We try to plug seekers into experiences of church that will restore dignity and meaning to their suffering, thereby ritualizing their reconciliation process.

But what about annulments? It may surprise you that within the framework of the kind of conversion process described thus far, annulments take on a different perspective for divorced Catholics. Perhaps in the past they have been marketed poorly as some kind of gimmick that provides loopholes for Catholics who don't value their marriage vows. We who minister must have a thorough understanding of what an annulment is and how local Tribunals process them. Given the true meaning of sacramental marriage, it becomes easier to understand the need for some kind of procedure to determine the sacramentality of a prior bond and the Tribunal's representation of the church in that procedure. There is great value in looking objectively at a broken marriage, not from a standpoint of right and wrong or good and bad, but in order to understand more clearly why the marriage failed. The time and introspection devoted to this reflection can be invaluable to healing, forgiving, and moving beyond the pain of divorce. Seekers who are afforded this opportunity through Tribunals that stress a ministerial approach tell of the new insights they gained not only about themselves but about their former partners as well. For many, it is a welcome closure to a pain-filled part of their lives. At last they are able to move past that pain. The self-knowledge gained through the annulment becomes invaluable to any future, sacramental bond.

We dispel all the myths listed earlier in this section with correct information and challenge the seekers to track down any outstanding myths that have been passed on to them as "absolute truth." Usually they return the following week with amusing stories of unfounded rumors. It is a time for all of us to laugh at ourselves a little and to acknowledge that the church does not do a very good job of informing us about these issues directly.

It is of primary importance to reinforce the fact that the annulment does not say there wasn't a marriage, because there was, and that the children are not made illegitimate by the annulment of a prior bond. These two issues again restore a semblance of credibility to the process. It is also important to clarify that the cost involved (average cost throughout the United States is $400) is not to purchase permission from Rome but to defray expenses. We have yet to meet a seeker who resented contributing toward the salaries of those who work for the church in the Tribunal offices, once they understand where their money goes.

Our own Tribunal experience is based on close contact with the Archdiocese of Saint Paul and Minneapolis, where a strong emphasis is placed on the ministerial aspect of the annulment process. The Tribunal trains a corps of "field advocates" who represent the petitioners and assist them in the preparation of their applications. We recommend that seekers avail themselves of one of these field advocates, rather than their pastors, to begin their annulment processes. We know the field advocates are committed to this ministry and that they understand every aspect of the Tribunal process. Unfortunately we have learned from experience that many parish priests do not know very much about these issues at all. Frankly, in this era of declining numbers of ordained clergy, it becomes a very reasonable alternative for the seeker to ask for help from among the nonordained who are trained and willing to give it.

While presenting our very positive experience with annulments, we must painfully and regretfully acknowledge that not every diocese in the United States provides the Catholic right to an annulment with the same kind of compassion and dignity that we describe. (Note that we use the word "right"; an annulment is not a privilege.) It is absolutely necessary that you talk with diocesan officials and come to a complete understanding of this process in your area before embarking on this outreach ministry to inactive Catholics. It will be even more helpful if members of your team become field advocates in those dioceses that offer such assistance to people seeking annulments.

If you discover that a judgmental, nonministerial attitude pervades your diocesan Tribunal, you may want to devote some attention and effort toward making it an opportunity for pastoral ministry and healing. It is unjust to subject anyone who has already endured the trauma of divorce to further grief and indignity, especially from the church, which is called to be the Body of Christ.

No discussion of annulments is complete without accurate information about the Internal Forum. The process just described is the External Forum and is the recommended option for annulment. While the External Forum rests within the entire church community, the Internal Forum deals only with the individual. It requires the cooperation of an ordained priest, mentor, or spiritual guide, and is handled on a one-to-one basis with the petitioner. It can be settled within the framework of the Sacrament of Reconciliation (Confession), although this is not always the case. As with the External Forum, it is imperative that the petitioner understand the process. Neither is a hocus-pocus, magic-wand solution; both are deeply rooted in church history and tradition, and both should be administered with charity, equity, and gentleness.

Father Barry Brunsman explains, "The exercise of Internal Forum by either clergy or laity usually takes a deeper faith and more maturity than exercise of the External Forum. Because it is personal, the responsibility for exercising it is assumed by the individual and not by church hierarchy or law. For this reason, the Internal Forum also goes under the name of 'good conscience,' 'good faith,' or 'pastoral care.' The Internal Forum honors the personal conscience of an individual—his or her honest appreciation of a life situation."[7]

It is the responsibility of the minister to emphasize the full responsibility of the individual in selecting this forum. We do not offer it as a easy solution or a quick resolution. Our approach is always to help the seeker assume his or her own responsibility for choices. To do less is to diminish their own dignity and to risk directing them into solutions that will only result in future confusion and guilt.

It is with deep, spiritual conviction that one should approach this forum in the process of annulling a marriage. A problem may arise in finding an ordained priest who is willing to participate in the forum with the same degree of commitment and conviction. Many are hesitant to participate at all; others feel it demands too much of their time; still others consider it an invalid process. It will be helpful for you to know priests in your diocese who are willing to implement this ministry and who will welcome your referrals. We do not recommend that you send seekers to their local pastor, or any other priest, unless you know how they will be received.

Having said this, we want to clarify that this forum is also the right of every Catholic, not just a privilege for some. As Father Brunsman states, this is the church's way of saying, "This is the law; now use good sense."

To clarify official church position on the Internal Forum, a directive from the Congregation of the Doctrine of the Faith was issued on April 11, 1973. It reaffirmed the church's teaching on indissolubility but reemphasized the necessity of pastoral care and compassion:

In regard to admission of the sacraments, local bishops are asked on the one hand to stress observance of current discipline, and on the other hand to take care that pastors of souls exercise special care to seek out those who are living in an irregular union by applying to the solution of such cases, in addition to other rightful means, the church's approved practice in the Internal Forum.

It becomes the responsibility of the petitioner and the priest to avoid scandal in the application of this forum. While this may seem trite in modern application, we know of horror stories about both parties of a broken marriage continuing to worship in the same parish community. You can imagine the resulting pain when one of those parties brings a new spouse into that community setting. Always we are to be motivated in our faith decisions by love of God and our neighbor, even our former spouse.

Whether presenting the Internal or External Forum, it is the minister's responsibility to explain the context, reasoning, and tradition in a way that respects the church's deep reverence for marriage and the seeker's right to prayerfully discern a proper course of direction. All of this takes time and, except for general information, is most effectively handled on an individual basis with the seeker. In no instance do we make recommendations based on loopholes and mechanical "how to's."

Sexual Issues

Because sexual issues are so numerous and so varied, we would like to provide you with some general background information. This will be helpful in the discussion of any sexual issues.

While often accusing church leaders of preoccupation with matters related to sex, the seekers also focus great concern on these issues. Their generally accepted understanding of what the church authorities teach regarding sex is "if it has to do with the body, the answer is no; don't do it."

Surrounding every issue—premarital sex, extramarital sex, masturbation, birth control, abortion, homosexuality, and AIDS—there is a sense that the authority in the church has broken into the bedroom and imposed its will on individuals and couples. This violation makes little sense to people who view their lives in terms of ongoing growth and awareness of themselves as wholly human, sexual beings. While Pope Paul VI's encyclical *Humanae Vitae* (*Of Human Life*), issued in 1968, contained rich, prosaic teachings on marriage and the relationship between husband and wife, it was interpreted by Catholic laity solely as a document that reiterated the ban on birth control. The beauty of the entire message was lost in the focus of the church's stand on that one issue.

And so another attempt by the hierarchy to enlighten and guide its community of faithful becomes an edict that is hopelessly out of touch with reality. Thus perceived, the church's teachings on matters relating to sex are often construed to be the result of the inability of those in authority, male celibates, to come to grips with their own sexuality. It is in this area, more than any other, that the hierarchy has lost credibility. We listen to painful accounts of the psychological consequences of the guilt and shame which were used to instill the church's moral teaching on young children. As adults, many cannot forgive the church for its legacy of fragmented and unhealthy concepts of human sexuality. Rather than sacred gift, these seekers find sex and sexuality permeated with feelings of guilt, shame, and sinfulness. Scars from childhood and teenage wounds heal slowly; there is risk in looking toward the church once again for direction in this vital area of their lives. Many are not interested in what the church has to say about sex at all.

While we hear statements such as "The church has no right to control or make judgments on how we are to express our sexuality," further discussion usually reveals that very few adult Catholics comprehend what the church really is saying about sex these days. Before we explore the particular issues that appear most often on our discussion agendas, it will be helpful to consider what the church is teaching and why it teaches what it does about human sexuality. Clear understanding of the sacredness of sexuality as an integral part of our humanity is essential if the seeker is to move beyond acceptance of rules and restrictions. Again, we consider the process of conversion to be exactly that—a *process* through which the seeker discovers the wholeness of his or her life in relationship to God and others. Incorporating one's sexuality into that process is an ongoing journey of discovery, especially if sex has been considered as something we *do*, instead of in the context of who we *are*.

Because the church's emphasis has been placed so strongly on individual deeds and sins, it is not surprising that the seekers focus on individual actions as well. Lost is the perspective of the whole, and with it, the moral values that underlie the teachings. Further, although the church has always taught about forgiveness and reconciliation, it is the areas relating to sex that, from the seekers' perspective, the church has been most unforgiving and most unwilling to offer reconciliation. It is as if these particular transgressions nullify the redemptive act of Christ; the church presents itself as incapable of extending partnership to those whose faith journeys cause them to explore and question these issues. Thus morality is perceived to rest solely on one's view of sex; transgressions of immorality in any other aspect of life can be forgiven—even understood—but defying the church's rigid rules pertaining to sex invokes an aura of damnation and elimination from the Body of Christ. It is a unique challenge to the minister to catalyze for the seekers the moral values that underlie centuries of distorted teaching practices, while at the same time, assuring them that in this area, as in any other of their lives as Christians, they are invited to explore, learn, and grow in the discernment of God's will for them.

It is our job to help the seekers understand that the church's teaching on sexuality is based on the premise that human sexuality touches every aspect of our existence. Young children, teenagers, adults, and senior citizens who are in loving relationship with one another and with God are affected by their sexuality. We are, by our very nature, sexual beings. We cannot deny this, and surprisingly enough, neither does the church. Since sexuality is of fundamental importance to each of us, it must be addressed in every stage of our personal development: as we must grow in our understanding of our developing intellect or emotional well-being, so must we be cognizant of our developing sexuality. In other words, to talk about our humanity or personhood, we must also talk about our sexuality. It is not a separate part of our existence that is less worthy than all the other miraculous components of our human lives. When the church reflects on human existence, it does so within a Christian context; therefore, the reflection will be different than a reflection from a totally secular context. The same is true when the church reflects on human sexuality. The ideals upheld will be different than those proposed by a purely secular consideration. The values are presented as ideals, based on the fulfillment of the Christian experience; it is naive to expect that everyone will achieve those ideals in this area of their lives or in any other. Still, the church upholds the ideals in order that we may continue to strive toward perfection and understanding of what it means to live as Christians. From this perspective, Christian values link human sexuality with two important goals: relationship and procreation.

Extremely helpful for both the minister and the seeker in providing a basis for discussion of particular sexual issues is a pastoral letter by Archbishop William Borders to the people of Baltimore. It was written as a clear, yet pastoral summary of the church's teaching on human sexuality. It provides a basis for discussion of the sexual issues that we will address. We quote from the pastoral:

The relational goal of human sexuality stresses the mutual love and concern between a man and woman in union with God. The procreational goal of human sexuality stresses the openness of every sexual act to the creation of new life and the mutual growth and support of the couple.[8]

Church teaching suggests that these goals of human sexuality can only be expressed properly and to their fullest in the sacramental union between husband and wife. When a couple enters a sacramental marriage, this human love and human union are given new depth and new meaning because they are placed within a spiritual context. Any sexual expression that is not open to the relational and procreational goals of human sexuality is considered incomplete and therefore wrong according to church teaching.

Loving relationships that are not open to the ideal goals of human sexuality, both relational and procreational, reject the sacramental essence of Christian love — for God and for one another. Sexual intercourse outside the context of marriage is not wrong simply because of an arbitrary rule. Instead, according to the church, it is wrong because it violates the ideals of Christian living and in the end, causes harm to one individual or the other. Archbishop Border's letter goes on to explain that the church considers three important components in determining its teaching on human sexuality:

BIOLOGICAL— This dimension of our sexuality is what we have in common with all life forms: reproduction.

PSYCHOLOGICAL— This dimension of our sexuality stresses our capacity to know and to love another. The psychological brings the biological to a new and deeper meaning.

SPIRITUAL— This dimension is the fullest level of our sexuality, for it places our sexuality in relationship with God. The knowing and loving of the psychological is united with our knowing and loving God.[9]

Each of these three dimensions of our sexuality is distinct. The church teaches that the three must always be linked together; they cannot be separated because they are aspects of the same reality within the same person. To view human sexuality as merely a matter of the biological or the psychological, and to miss the reality of the deepest spiritual dimension, would be a fragmented understanding of it. It removes sexuality from the wholeness of our lives. The church teaches that sin arises from the attempt to view sexuality from only one dimension. With these three dimensions in mind, let's look at the specific human sexuality issues that cause most concern for the seekers.

Sex Before/Outside Marriage

Seekers' Perspective

- "I'm not ready to settle down and get married; I have to finish school, find a job. Sex is a natural part of life. What's the big deal?"
- "We've been engaged for over a year; sex has become a natural expression of our love for one another. We've already made a commitment which we intend to live out for the rest of our lives."
- "Our marriage has been empty for years. We just live together, with no love or sharing between us. What happens to the kids if we get a divorce? There's hardly enough money to go around now. We stopped having sex years ago; it was empty and horrible for both of us. But I can't live as a celibate and the church doesn't condone divorce and remarriage. I can only see two choices: break up my family or have these occasional affairs. The church says both are wrong, so how can I win?"

Church's Perspective

The church is clear on these issues: there must be a stable bond and a permanent commitment between a man and woman in sacramental marriage in order for sexual expression to be acceptable. Without that bond and commitment, there can be no assurance of sincerity or fidelity. Sexual expression void of true commitment does not offer protection for potential new life, nor for the two partners to encourage one another's growth for the rest of their lives through mutual support and love. The church sees any sexual relationship that does not fulfill these criteria as one that reduces human sexuality to the purely biological and psychological dimension. The spiritual dimension of human sexuality has been set aside, creating a fragmentation that falls short of the Christian ideal of wholeness. Literally, the church calls this "sin."

Pastoral Perspective

Reality, however, tells us that many men and women find it as impossible to live up to this ideal of sexuality as it is in any other aspect of their lives. We neither condone, nor make judgments. It is not our job to give permission or to prescribe further action. Rather we present the church's teaching on human sexuality, not in a negative or punitive light but as an opportunity for heightened awareness of the sacredness of one's total human sexuality.

We invite the seekers to respond to this heightened awareness, realizing that for many, it is just the beginning of a process. It is the first time that some seekers have heard what the church is *really* saying underneath all those rigid rules. They have a chance to stop and reflect on their lives and their relationships. While not everyone can accept the church teaching, many begin to see every aspect of their sexuality in a new light. We stress that the church's requirement of openness to life requires more than the minimal concept of "having babies." It is the absolute necessity that our sexual relationships include the respect for the sacredness of the life of each partner—the health, wholeness, and dignity of each. This is the epitome of Christian sexual relationship, a far cry from sex for the sake of sex and a long way from the currently pervading societal concept of sexuality.

When we present this new way to consider their own specific situations, the seekers are allowed to consider their lives and their choices from a different stance, one of interior commitment rather than ignorant obedience to something that makes no sense to them. We continue to support, encourage, and guide them as they seek their own moral truths, guided by a new awareness of their personal moral convictions and the values that underlie the church's teaching.

Masturbation

Seekers' Perspective

- "I can't believe the church is really concerned about this anymore! It's a phase people go through."
- "As soon as I reached puberty, I knew I was in trouble. I had to confess this over and over again. I felt ashamed and dirty and now I resent the church for making me feel that way about something that was so normal for a child."
- "Are we supposed to believe that celibates don't masturbate? Why do we all have to feel so sneaky about this?"
- "Doesn't the church have something more to do than create nightmares for teenagers?"
- "Why doesn't the church take seriously some of the input from social and psychological disciplines on masturbation? We're not living in the Dark Ages!"

Church's Perspective

The church still considers masturbation a sin, especially if it becomes a substitute for a deep and abiding relationship. The church says that the act itself, lacking the relational and procreational goals of sexuality, has little true sexual meaning and is therefore usually associated with some degree of sexual immaturity. It falls short of the ideal.

Pastoral Perspective

Many seekers have resolved this issue for themselves, during their own process of maturity. But the scars from all of those negative judgments, without any positive guidance or teaching during budding awareness of sexuality, are deep. Our approach is to open up these dark areas for discussion, where feelings can be shared with one another and experiences can be evaluated from a new perspective. Exposed to this kind of scrutiny, childhood nightmares can be replaced with increased self-awareness and compassion. But it is the minister's responsibility to offer new perspectives from which to consider the concept of masturbation and its place in an individual's life. For those for whom it has become more than a "healthy release," or "natural outlet," it is sometimes necessary to help them see that blaming the church allows them to avoid taking responsibility to mature and grow in their understanding of their sexuality, indeed their personhood. Obviously some of this work must be done on a one-to-one basis, where confidentiality is respected and trust between the minister and the seeker is strongly developed. The minister must discern whether or not outside counseling resources should be recommended in those cases where the residual effects of shame and guilt have literally paralyzed the seeker into a position of sexual inertia or deviation.

In most cases, however, this issue becomes a nonissue, as we accept our humanity and understand that the church, as well as the rest of society, is in the process of learning more and more about healthy sexuality. Referencing individual acts of masturbation within the full spectrum of healthy Christian sexuality gives the seeker a new basis from which to determine his or her own direction.

Birth Control

Seekers' Perspective

- "The pope doesn't have the slightest idea what he is talking about. If he was married and had to practice what he preaches, he would quickly change his mind."
- "What do celibates really know about loving intimacy and the role that sex plays in marriage? What about the effects of too many children on the primary relationship of the husband and wife—or for that matter, on the kids themselves?"
- "Anyway, most Catholics are practicing birth control. Who is fooling whom?"
- "It is irresponsible for the pope to be telling Third World nations that they need more babies! What about overpopulation, poverty, food shortages? It is hard to accept what the church teaches about justice and human rights when it is leading these developing nations into deeper poverty and turmoil by its outdated theology of procreation!"
- "For twenty-five years, I thought I would go to hell because we simply could not risk having more children. We could hardly handle the eight we have. I haven't received the sacraments at any of my own kids' weddings because I thought I was such a sinner. Now I can't believe I let a priest who didn't even know what a good person I am judge me like that. How do I undo all those years of feeling unacceptable in God's eyes? I know now that God knew we were doing the best we could!"
- "My mother died while giving birth to her twelfth child. I was her oldest child and suddenly became a mother to all those kids when I was only fifteen years old. Don't tell me about birth control!"

Church's Perspective

The prohibition of the use of birth control for Catholics was reaffirmed by *Humane Vitae,* which included the following statement: "each and every act of marriage must remain open to the transmission of life."[10] In other words, authentic sexual expression that takes place within a sacramental marriage must always be open to the creation of new life. Any means to interrupt or prevent life is unacceptable. In more recent years, Pope John Paul II has reinforced this teaching.

Pastoral Perspective

There are some people who agree fully with *Humane Vitae*'s interpretation of authentic sexual expression. Others have found total peace, even enrichment in their lives and their marriages through the use of Natural Family Planning. Certainly it is the minister's task to offer every possible encouragement to do so. Many dioceses have active Natural Family Planning organizations and their programs are extremely helpful to couples who seek to resolve this issue in full compliance of church teaching.[11] These groups emphasize the sacredness of marriage and the involvement of both partners in the planning of their families. It is deeply rooted in mutual respect and prayer.

There are other Catholics, however, who do not find the answer in the stated church teaching, nor in Natural Family Planning. Consider those marriages where only one partner is committed to these solutions, or where these solutions fail to resolve the reality of too many children at the wrong time in a marriage. There are those who take seriously *Humanae Vitae*'s call to "responsible parenthood" and the individual couple's decision in conscience to determine the full extent of what that responsibility entails. Large numbers of Catholics support theologians' or bishops' conferences that hold for a broader interpretation of authentic human sexuality. They would see *Humanae Vitae* as stressing too strongly the spiritual and procreational goals of sexuality at the expense of the relational goals of the marriage itself.

Applied on the practical level, Catholics throughout the world (Germany, France, Canada, United States) have been encouraged and supported by their bishops in their discernment process. If Catholics strive to understand and live out the church's teaching regarding birth control, but find it difficult, they are reassured with compassion and understanding from their bishops who say "that they should not consider that because of this inability that they are separated from God's love through mortal sin."[12]

This is the encouragement we offer to seekers who struggle with the application of this teaching to their lives. In making their decision about birth control, we suggest they search out the church's teaching and discuss it with a church representative who will guide them in their discernment. We remind them that prayer does help in this process and that the Holy Spirit will be present to them, even to those who ultimately choose less than the ideal offered by the church.

Abortion

Seekers' Perspective

- "Why can't the church forgive me? It was wrong, but I was young. I can't undo what I did. How do I live without the promise of forgiveness for murdering my child? I cannot let go of the horror of that act, but where do I go to find peace? Where is the loving, forgiving God the church talks about? Not in the Catholic church! Is this the only unforgivable sin?"

- "Why wasn't the church there for me when I was pregnant, filled with shame and guilt? I was afraid to tell anyone, even my parents; I was so ashamed."

- "What right does the church have to tell me what I can and cannot do with my body? I have a right to decide. Besides, the church can't even agree on when an embryo becomes a human being."

- "The church says you can kill in what they call a just war. What if this pregnancy is life threatening to the mother?"

- "Why doesn't the church zero in more on the men who walk out on the lives of these mothers and their babies? Isn't that abandoning life too? Why is all the shame heaped on the woman who feels trapped into this decision?"

- "This is simply an emotional issue; these people rant and rave about abortion while some of them see nothing wrong with capital punishment. Where's the consistency in that?"

Church's Perspective

The church's prohibition of abortion for any reason is deeply rooted in its early formation. The one value that underlies all Christian teaching is sacredness of life. In 1974 the church re-affirmed its position on abortion as follows:

The first right of the human person is the right to life. . . . Hence it must be protected above all the others. It does not belong to society, nor does it belong to public authority in any form to recognize this right for some and not for others: all discrimination is evil, whether it be founded on race, sex, color, or religion. It is not recognition by another that constitutes this right. This right is antecedent to its recognition; it demands recognition and it is strictly unjust to refuse it. . . . The right to life remains complete in an old person, even one greatly weakened, it is not lost by one who is incurably sick. The right to life is no less to be respected in the small infant just born than in the mature person. In reality, respect for human life is called for from the time that the process of generation begins. From the time that the ovum is fertilized, a life is begun which is neither that of the father nor of the mother; it is rather the life of a new human being with his or her own growth.[13]

It is alarming to many Catholics that the church prohibits abortion even in those cases when the mother's life is in danger. The emphasis on the sacredness of human life is extended to all humans at all times. In principle, this means that neither the life of the mother, nor the child, can be subjected to an act of direct suppression in order to save the other. In all situations, Catholics are obliged to make every effort to save both lives. In stark reality, this can be a grim teaching.

Pastoral Perspective

Again, using the church's declaration as a teaching tool, we gain some insights about our response to the dilemma of abortion in our society. This teaching is a challenge and admonishment to the entire Christian community, not only those faced with the immediate resolution of a pregnancy:

Every man and woman with feeling, and certainly every Christian, must be ready to do what they can to remedy the [sorrows and miseries which cause people to choose abortion]. . . . One can never approve of abortion; but it is above all necessary to combat its causes, . . . to do everything possible to help families, mothers, and children.[14]

Within this context of community responsibility, it is more difficult to wield judgment solely on those who may be the greatest victims of abortion—the women who have had them. We are all too aware of the singularly heavy load of guilt that has been placed on them. When we discuss this issue in our group settings, we invite the seekers to discuss the kinds of desperation that often lead one to make that decision, and the lack of cultural and church support available to most women during those times. We keep the ideal, the concept of the sacredness of all human life, in the fore of these discussions in order to promote comparisons of that ideal with prevailing societal and cultural attitudes. This very sacredness is also each individual's assurance of forgiveness by a compassionate God and a loving church community.

It is important during these group discussions that the invitation is held out frequently to anyone who would like to make a one-to-one appointment to discuss the matter further. It is unfair to encourage a woman who is grappling with the enormity of this issue on a very personal level to discuss it in these group settings. These private sessions are very different than the group discussions on abortion. The pain is personal. The issue is not simply a teaching or dogma; it is monumental to the individual seeker's life and her relationship with God. To put it simply and tragically, these are often women whose guilt has never allowed them to grieve the loss of their babies, nor to forgive themselves.

We encourage long, quiet talks about the events of their lives that led up to the abortion, encouraging them to analyze their choice through the perspective of time and increased understanding. We talk about grief and encourage them to embrace the same kind of healing through grief that we would encourage for any woman who loses a baby through miscarriage. Over and over again, we point out the goodness that we see evidenced in their lives, and the cherishment that God feels for them. It is especially helpful, when the seeker feels she is ready, to refer her to an understanding priest who will guide her through a deeply spiritual experience of sacramental reconciliation. It is often necessary to help them find sensitive counseling by therapists who understand the devastation experienced by so many women who have had abortions, Catholic or not.

Abortion may be part of a much larger picture of unresolved issues, including dysfunctional families of origin, lack of self-esteem, behavior compulsions, and other symptoms of unsuccessful lives. As with any other issue the seekers bring to us, even abortion then becomes the catalyst to growth, self-understanding, and ongoing conversion in the seeker's relationship with God. Given permission to bring God deeply into the process of their healing, these women evidence powerful sensitivity and compassion toward others, as their own wounds heal. Some of them are actually called through their brokenness and healing to minister to others, and their ministry is powerful.

We are thankful that so many bishops are including in their

offices of pastoral ministries post-abortion counseling teams that offer sensitive, professional counseling to women and men who live with the heavy weight of this issue on their consciences. We, as church, are learning valuable lessons from these women, especially some in their eighties, as they share their long-kept secrets of painful self-incrimination. Whenever possible, we refer seekers who are directly dealing with this issue to such ministries. It is especially healing to be embraced, nurtured, and loved in this process by the church.

Still unresolved and open to much debate within the church is the issue of whether a person can be prochoice and remain Catholic. The official church has been very public in its criticism of those who profess to be both. There is little we can say to the seekers that will provide an immediate solution to this dilemma. We can only provide a place to continue the discussion in an atmosphere of mutual respect.

Homosexuality

Seekers' Perspective

- "I can't help it. I am gay. God made me this way."
- "What am I supposed to do about my sexuality, my loneliness, my need for intimacy?"
- "I used to think gays were weird; then I found out my favorite brother is gay. We've gotten so close since he told me. His life has been horrible because of something he can't help. I cannot judge him anymore, so how can I judge any of the others?"
- "We are not being promiscuous; our commitment to one another is permanent and we are faithful to each other, so why doesn't the church accept us? Can God accept us, even if the church can't?"
- "The church says it's all right to be lesbian, but not to

express my sexuality. But our sexuality is a part of who we are. If this is the way I was created, how can it be wrong to express it?"

- "The pope says all gays and lesbians should be celibate. He made a free choice to be celibate and now he tells us that we have no choice. Gay Catholics are forced to be more celibate than some of the clergy who took vows to be celibate. They don't get kicked out of the church!"

Church's Perspective

The church's condemnation of expressed homosexuality dates back to pre-Christian biblical tradition. Currently the controversy regarding homosexuality is not limited to the Catholic church or to Christianity; it is widespread throughout our culture, with people of opposing views from all walks of life. Consistent in its teaching that every sexual expression must be open to the creation of new life, and because homosexual expression precludes the possibility of procreational aspects of human sexuality, the church says that it is not an authentic expression of true sexuality. The church does contend, however, that every person—including the homosexual—needs to be nourished and accepted within the community of the faithful. Because they are created by God, and because all life is sacred, homosexuals are of value and importance to the life of the church. The big "if" that follows is "as long as they remain celibate."

Pastoral Perspective

It is impossible to minister to gay and lesbian Catholics without identifying with the strong feeling of rejection that most of them receive from the church. While they are supposed to celebrate their sacredness in God's eyes and in the eyes of the church community, their experience is a very conditional kind of acceptance, unlike that meted out to other saints and sinners who make up the Body of Christ. Our pastoral attention is drawn to the rejection they experience, not only toward their sexual identity but to their human existence. We have not found a satisfactory way to explain the church's stance to these hurting men and women. How can we express the church's love and care for them, when the church applies different parameters to their sexuality than to everyone else? If our sexuality is central to our humanity, is it not so for the homosexual as well?

The very admission of this confusion within our own hearts can build bridges between the homosexual seekers and the part of church that we represent. We clearly distinguish the difference between God's love and acceptance and that offered by church authorities. We acknowledge, but do not take responsibility for, the fact that there are those within the church who cannot see the sacredness and goodness that God sees in everyone, whether they are heterosexual or homosexual. We try to convey God's love and compassion through our own caring respect for the valid struggle that faces every gay and lesbian Catholic. We acknowledge that it may be through that struggle, empowered by the Holy Spirit, that the church and all its members will be brought to a greater realization of God's truth. We also attempt to help these people connect with positive church and worship experiences, relationships within the church that will be nourishing and affirming to them in their quest for authentic spiritual identity. But most of the time this doesn't seem like enough. We are often left wanting, knowing only too well that to these people, the church doors seem rather firmly closed.

AIDS (Acquired Immune Deficiency Syndrome)

Seekers' Perspective

- "This is a life-and-death issue and the church reduces it to whether or not someone uses condoms!"
- "The church makes me feel like God is punishing me because I am gay."

- "I'm gay; finally the church cares about me — because I have AIDS!"

Church's Perspective

As in all aspects of our society, the church has been confronted with the enormity of this issue without adequate time for thorough reflection. Statistics indicate that AIDS will be a continuing concern for all of society. In November 1989, the American bishops issued a statement titled *Called to Compassion and Responsibility: A Response to the HIV/AIDS Crises.*[15] In this pastoral letter, they urged compassion and understanding for all "people with AIDS" (PWA). They rejected any AIDS testing for discriminatory purposes and questioned the need for widespread, mandatory testing. They criticized the refusal of medical and dental treatment for PWA and called for the private and public funding of AIDS research and education.

Among the bishops themselves, the initial draft of this pastoral caused controversy over whether or not the use of condoms should be encouraged in AIDS prevention and education programs. Nonetheless the final draft supported those bishops who steadfastly maintained that the only way to prevent the spread of this disease was through total sexual abstinence. What is interesting about this pastoral letter is that the public attention and debate, both within the church and the private sector, focused on the use of condoms rather than the compassion called for in the document.

Pastoral Perspective

We need to acknowledge the seriousness of this issue; sooner or later it will touch all of our lives. That fact alone evokes a feeling of solidarity with PWA. As Jesus did, we need to respond to the problem as it exists and be open to information from other disciplines and teachers.

The church's official stand regarding the effectiveness of condoms in preventing or slowing down the spread of this disease does cause legitimate concern for public health officials and those segments of the population hardest hit by AIDS. While the debate regarding condoms continues, local churches, clergy, and laity are pioneering effective, compassionate ministries to PWA and their families. Ordained clergy and pastoral ministers are teaming up with health-care professionals to provide lasting, comprehensive care that includes the inner healing of PWA and those in sphere of relationship to them. Their work produces stress and feelings of futility because of the enormity and complexity of the problem. We have seen Christ most vividly in the lives of the dedicated people who minister in this way. The power of the Holy Spirit to call forth individual response is evident in this growing movement within the church community, with and without the endorsement and consent of church authorities. Those who minister to PWA tell of the powerful inner conversion that takes place in the lives of many who prepare to meet their God in death. Often their lives become heroic stories of faith and courage to the community as a whole.

The underlying values that support the church's teaching need to be fostered in ways that convey an understanding of wholeness and healthy human sexuality. AIDS challenges us as church to present these values in a manner that recognizes the sacredness of human sexuality and the sacredness of one another. As church, we must respond with compassion to the problems that unfold regarding the AIDS crisis. To do less will only produce another category of hurting, angry, inactive Catholics.

Women's Issues

Seekers' Perspective

- "It is a contradiction for the male-dominated church authority to preach human justice and dignity while denying women ministerial equality because Jesus was a male!"

- "How can a church maintain relevancy to a modern world with its archaic concept of a woman's role?"

- "Every time the Vatican speaks out on this issue, it gets worse. Frankly I'm embarrassed to belong to a church that is so reflective of the Dark Ages."

- "God is conceptualized as a father; women are denied equal opportunity to respond to their baptismal call to serve in the church; canon law says women cannot serve at the altar, even as lectors! Men make the rules; men carry out the rules; men enforce the rules. Yet they perpetuate the myth of 'Holy Mother, the church.' In reality it is 'Holy Father, the church!'"

- "The whole mood of Holy Week was destroyed by the bishop's insistence that women could not participate in the foot-washing ceremony. How in the world does he reflect Christ to anyone, much less the female members of the Catholic community?"

- "This whole thing smacks more of power and ignorance than anything spiritual. Think of the difference in church we would all be experiencing today if women had been included as equals."

- "As a father and a husband, I cannot sit back and accept the church's limitations on opportunities for women to participate."

- "Another generation of children, both boys and girls, is being affected by the church's outmoded concept of male/female roles. While the reality is that most women no longer have the choice to stay home and nurture families, the pope is still telling society that her primary role is to be a wife and mother."

- "Even as a workplace, the church falls behind the secular world in its unfair treatment, abuse, and exploitation of women."

Church's Perspective

In March 1984, the American bishops invited women from all walks of life to meet with them in small groups where they could discuss women-related issues in the church. Each group was invited to summarize their issues, good and bad, in order to make recommendations that would affect the content of a bishops' pastoral letter on women. A drafting committee received feedback from one hundred dioceses, representing all regions of the country, totaling responses from approximately seventy-five thousand women. While innovative in its preparation procedure, the resulting document, *Partners in the Mystery of Redemption: A Pastoral Response to Women's Concerns for Church and Society,*[16] did not do enough. While it defined sexism as sin, many see the document as perpetuating the continuation of sexism in the church.

In *The Dignity of Women,* Pope John Paul II reaffirmed a male-only priesthood. He pointed out that Christ often contradicted the culture of his times in stressing the equal dignity of men and women before God. He went on to say that the church has always recognized the "feminine genius" and encourages women as mothers and consecrated religious to contribute to social and church development. Many heard in that apostolic letter a reaffirmation of the age-old concept that consecrated virginity is a superior state of life. The document concludes with acknowledgment of the perfect woman as one who "becomes an irreplaceable support and source of strength for other people."[17]

Pastoral Perspective

Before we can possibly minister to others who are smarting from this issue, we must painfully scrutinize the implications of these teachings in our individual lives in the church and to our own resolution of the injustice. To a generation of women tenaciously fighting to overcome the debilitating effects of codependency, the contents of *The Dignity of Women* were not welcomed. It does little good to diminish the severity of the church's teachings; seekers are more informed on this than any other controversial issue in the American church. Nor can we whitewash these teachings by stressing the contribution of women in life of the church. What the seekers want to talk about is the contribution of the church in the life of its women! While many women continue to work toward change within the institutional church, growing numbers simply wear out and leave. Others revert to more radical means to achieve change. It is obvious that among women themselves there is no single approach to the resolution of this dilemma.

Since we find little encouragement from the institutional church, we remind seekers that there is hope in the message of Jesus:

The social situation of first century Palestine in which women were, in fact, the chattel property of their husbands, and the religious situation in which women had but limited access to the temple precincts sufficiently bespeak the fact that women were generally considered inferior to men. In this respect, women were on the fringes of society. They were an alienated group within their homeland. Within this set of circumstances, Jesus' attitude toward women and his ministry to them is particularly significant. . . . His ministry to women was an element of the scandal of the coming of the kingdom.[18]

That is where we begin—with Jesus. It is impossible to defend the injustice; more education is not needed. The facts speak for themselves. There may be some merit in considering with the seekers women's role in secular culture and finding injustice there as well. However the response is usually, "But, the church should lead society in fighting injustice; instead it rationalizes injustice because society has failed to grant women basic human dignity."

For every woman who struggles with her own faith commitment, her own connectedness to the goodness within the Body of Christ called church, there is the daily confrontation with the reality of what too often amounts to actual abuse by her church. That reality has to be acknowledged and validated for the seeker. Whether or not she can sustain that emotional and spiritual bombardment depends largely on the amount of spiritual and emotional support available to her from others within the church who see this wrong for what it is.

It is asking a lot of a woman to suggest that she "stay in and work toward change." Only those who have suffered the injustice of second-class citizenship in any society understand the daily pressure such a decision entails. Her focus must rest clearly on goals that are real and valuable to her, but probably not attainable in her lifetime. Without such a focus, she begins to feel like a pawn in a system that considers its own end at her expense. It is almost impossible to maintain a healthy emotional and spiritual equilibrium once there is an awareness of our being used by the system. Carolyn Osiek, in her book *Beyond Anger*, says of such an awareness:

Life is not as it was before, and can never be so again. It cannot return to the comfort of denial. One's self-image of loyalty and one's experience of oppression come to a screeching collision with one another and seem henceforth incompatible. How can I remain loyal to a person, institution, or tradition that has done this to me? But without that commitment, what do I have left? Who am I?[19]

While we have to accept the reality of the status quo, there are discussions that prove helpful in stirring the embers of hope. Too often the issue of women in the church centers on the issue of ordination. Pro and con discussions, rationalizations, and obvious arguments for such ordination bear little fruit. On the other hand, we encourage the seekers to consider the role of priesthood itself. Can it possibly continue in its present form in light of the catapulting decrease of its members? Would the Holy Spirit really allow the church to disappear because ordained priesthood as we know it becomes impossible, due to lack of interest? Exploration of the history of ministry in the church helps the seeker see hope in the possibility that a change in the structure of priesthood itself may be the necessary prerequisite to a priesthood of service rather than power, whether the priest is woman or man. Good background material is found in Dominican Thomas Franklin O'Meara's *Theology of Ministry,* in which he states, "The context of a theology of ministry for today is not decline, but expansion."[20] What a hopeful message for those of us, men and women, called by our baptism to service within the church. In O'Meara's clear overview of the development of ministry over the two-century experience of church, we find great hope for the future. It is a strength of the Catholic church that the perspective of history frequently gives us insights into the working of the Holy Spirit and instills hope for the future.

Building on that hope, it is also helpful to enlighten the seekers to the great expanse of ministry that is available to women, indeed to all in the church, aside from that of ordained priest. At a recent Celebration of Ministry sponsored by the Archdiocese of St. Paul and Minneapolis, more than six hundred ministers of the church gathered to hear Bishop Robert Morneau in a presentation called "Called and Gifted: Discovering, Freeing, Celebrating." Few of those attending this affirming, positive experience of church were men; fewer still were ordained. The sheer number of women whose ministerial gifts were being celebrated that day provided an aura of hope for all who attended. For those of us grown weary with the struggle, it was a day filled with hope and promise.

It is helpful, too, to discuss the differences in the giftedness that men and women bring to the ministry of priesthood. There is a prevailing movement among inactive female Catholics that seems to speak of the superiority of female leadership, based on gender alone. We encourage the seekers to talk about a scenario where a powerful, male-dominated priesthood is replaced by a powerful, female-dominated priesthood. It quickly becomes evident that the solution is not as simple as replacing one gender with another but rather with a renewed understanding of priesthood. Such discussions, in a reverent, respect-filled format, are invaluable; they help the seekers find words to validate their personal experience of church and to name their hopes for the future. For many of us who stay and commit ourselves toward ridding the church of injustice of any form, there is the hope of our children knowing a different kind of church, one more closely resembling that Kingdom which Jesus has called us all to build with him. There is great dignity in aligning ourselves with the women and men of the ages who have dared to dream, to hope, and to work for change, albeit at great cost and personal sacrifice. It is that ultimate dignity to which we call the seeker.

Male team members play a vital role in ministering to these seekers. Women who agonize over their restricted role in the church are often surprised to discover how deeply this issue touches the lives of men as well. A word of caution, however: while it may be helpful to clarify for the seekers our own reasons for remaining in the church, it cannot be presumed that they will be able to make the same decision. Our role is to help them in the choosing of a direction that will restore peace and hope to their journeys of faith.

Changes

Seekers' Perspective

- "It just isn't the same church I belonged to when I was growing up."
- "Why are they so secretive about all the changes? How are we supposed to know what they are or why they changed everything?"
- "This is the first place I have found since Vatican II where we can learn what went on there!"

- "They just changed too much, too fast."
- "Why didn't they go further? They just scratched the surface."
- "What happened to all those people who went to hell for eating meat on Fridays?"
- "Why do they call the mass 'Eucharist?' The priest used to be in charge there; now there are all kinds of people up there on Sunday mornings. I've seen flutes, drums—even dancers—on the altar. Where will it stop?"
- "Why can't women preach; why can't girls be altar servers?"
- "The mass seems so Protestant now; what's the difference, anyhow?"

Church's Perspective

In the past many Catholics were taught an absolute and eternal "rightness" of the church's laws and practices. The primary virtue was obedience, acceptance of what we were told. As Catholics we were taught not to challenge or question anything. Many of these practices and teachings were the result of cultural, political, and historical situations and had little connection with fundamental Catholic teaching. The initial response to Vatican II was an abrupt change in the external identity of church: Latin to English, the altar turned around, participatory liturgies, and the actual removal from sanctuaries of the statues, altars, and artwork that designated a church "Catholic." In reality Vatican II was much more, and it is the depth of that Council's teachings that is now permeating the church, albeit a quarter of a century later. The thrust of Vatican II was not one of uncontrolled reform, but of restoration. It called the church and its members to inner renewal, a return to religious worship, piety, and spirituality characteristic of the early church. However, most of the changes have been imposed with very little education, explanation, or communication. The result is an entire generation of Catholics who are left bewildered and insecure by the church's new mode of spiritual direction.

Pastoral Perspective

Because of the strong feelings of some that the church has changed too much, and by others that the church has not changed nearly enough, the discussions on change may become heated. To avoid discounting one another's feelings, we remind the seekers that our invitation to share honestly is conditioned on our mutual respect for one another. This is a good opportunity to point out that the church is composed of people at different stages of faith development, from different cultural backgrounds, and from a spectrum of ages, genders, and lived experience. It is natural, therefore, that there will be varying likes and dislikes. We state our conviction that the Catholic church is big enough for all of us, even if we have different feelings, issues, and experiences of God.

It is helpful to invite the seekers to express their feelings of confusion, anger, and fear about all this change in the church they thought would always be the same. Allow them to tell their stories of pastors who, in carrying out Vatican II injunctions, arbitrarily changed comfortable church surroundings into sterile worship "halls," void of any symbolic connection to God in the minds of parishioners. Other pastors assumed a position of defiance against all change, teaching their flocks that the old way was the right way. For the first time, Catholics were caught up in confusion as church leaders actually disagreed among themselves. Those bad feelings are still there and need to be expressed. Parishes are still divided, living legacies of bitterness and anger, rather than being communities of love and acceptance.

There is another group, even larger in number, who come to us because of what they call a "breath of fresh air" provided by Vatican II. They welcome the new vitality and vigor it brought to the church, but they complain that renewal seems to have come to a standstill, and that the changes don't reach far enough. There is nothing more debilitating than hope raised in vain. Catholics who welcome the openness and self-scrutiny that began in the church after Vatican II resent the return to an authoritarian structure that once again idealizes obedience to the law, rather than to one's heart. This reversal is a troubling reality to a large, new group of Catholics, and they are leaving the church because of it. They express their frustration with resignation: "It was bad enough before, when we didn't know anything else; now we are being suffocated by the church's out-of-date edicts. We can't go back to the old way of doing things." These seekers see the momentum of reform and positive change slowing down drastically; some say it has stopped with John Paul II. They worry that all the positive effects of Vatican II will be lost and are worried about the future of the church as it loses relevance to a world that needs to focus on the future, not the past.

As facilitator and team, it will be helpful for you to understand these strong, often opposing reactions to change that will surface at your sessions. It is essential that you reflect on your own experience of change and how it has affected your life as a Catholic. It is difficult to minister to seekers who are distressed by an issue that actually pleases the minister. We need to identify our biases and our own strong feelings about these issues in order to treat each seeker with openness and acceptance of individual issues. If we cut off their discussions by rationalization or teaching, the seekers may never have another opportunity to bring these confusing issues into the open where they can heal.

Ironically, because of these indepth discussions, both groups of seekers—those who value change and those who resent it—frequently tell us that for the first time in their adult experience, they are able to hear opinions of Catholics on "the other side" of this issue without feeling threatened or angry. Arbitrary positions of "too much" or "not enough" change are often softened by the unconditional support and acceptance of one another that permeates these gatherings. Sides are less likely to be drawn up if we are not going to be ridiculed for saying what we feel and believe. Gradually it becomes evident that we all have a place in the church, whatever our views on these issues.

Already bonded to one another by their alienation, seekers who come to our meetings begin to realize that the church is composed of many different types of people. Since they are already feeling comfortable in a group representative of varying attitudes about change in the church, it becomes easier to accept the notion of a truly universal church — indeed one that encourages diversity. We encourage the seekers to see the church from a global perspective; it becomes obvious to them that a burning need for change in our country may not even be a concern for a local church on another continent. It helps them to see the need for the universal church to remain keenly aware of the impact of its teachings on cultures ranging from very primitive to our own technologically advanced society.

While consideration of the universal aspect of church does allow us to understand why the church changes and why it may not change fast enough, it does not solve the problem. It is our task, as facilitators, to dwell on the traditional, biblical, and historical legacy that has always allowed the church to adapt to diverse cultures in different ways, at different times. This is what being Catholic is all about. It has only been in our most recent history that we have perceived ourselves as "cookie-cutter Catholics," all stamped out of one mold.

Change is difficult for most human beings. However, it would be unfair to encourage anyone to reconcile with a church imagined to be rigid and unchanging in light of the vast potential for change that is looming on the immediate horizon. Change is a necessary part of growth. As Jesus taught us, there can be no transformation without change. New life is only possible after death. Most seekers recognize the vast amount of change that has taken place in all other areas of their lives. We help them to integrate their perceptions of church into their entire lived experience and in doing so, change becomes a natural part of their Catholic experience. Rather than asking the seeker if change is good or bad, our questions should focus on "How much change are you willing to accept?" or "How quickly should the church make changes?"

We invite the seekers to struggle along with us in the ongoing formation of church as we face issues of increased lay involvement, shortages of clergy, and redefined concepts of sacramental celebration. Changes will continue to happen; if not, the very future of the church could be in jeopardy. To embrace the need for change and our struggle as an ongoing battle of a decaying church would be to miss the point completely. Rather, that very struggle is a sign of life, of the Spirit at work in our midst, of people responding to their baptismal calls. Our role is to challenge the seekers to accept the struggle as reality and to see in it a hopeful sign of a church that is truly alive.

Confession

Seekers' Perspective

- "I still have nightmares about that black box; it is one of my most terrifying childhood memories."
- "It seemed so phony—rattling off all those Our Fathers and Hail Marys even though I knew I'd be back in another week or two to list the same sins and receive the same penance."
- "Confession conjures up images of angry priests, fires of hell, God's wrath. I just can't do it anymore."
- "It's the first Catholic thing that I quit doing and I quit as soon as I moved away from my parents."
- "Why can't I go directly to God? Who needs that torture box?"

Church's Perspective

Of all the changes implemented by Vatican II, perhaps none was more welcome than those surrounding the Sacrament of

Confession. Even the new name of this sacrament, *reconciliation,* signifies the depth of these changes. Millions of active Catholics have abandoned completely the practice of going to weekly confession. Along with our seekers, they may not even recognize the Sacrament of Reconciliation as it is celebrated today. It has truly become a celebration of God's forgiveness. To describe confession in terms of celebration would seem to be a contradiction to many. But it is an indication of how drastically the sacrament has changed. Gone is the black box; in its place there is free-flowing prayer and dialogue between the priest and penitent.

To heighten awareness of the communal aspect of sin and forgiveness, Vatican II offered two additional forms of the Sacrament of Reconciliation. The original form of reconciliation is the most familiar; it consists of individual confession and absolution (words of God's forgiveness) between the priest and penitent. A new form that has become popular in some dioceses and churches during special times of the year (Advent or Lent) is a gathering of a large number of people in the church for communal prayers, music, and Scripture. This is followed by individual confession of sins and absolution.

Another new form of reconciliation is used only in special circumstances defined by the local bishop (emergencies, disasters, or when the number of people in attendance is too great or the time necessary to properly celebrate the sacrament is too long). This form of reconciliation includes general confession of sins and general absolution.

Clearly the church stresses that it is God who forgives sins, but the church also teaches that sin affects our relationships with one another. As did the early Christians, we need to acknowledge our sinfulness and request forgiveness from one another. In reconciliation, the priest represents the community while sharing God's healing with the penitent. It is that healing which the sacrament celebrates.

Pastoral Perspective

In any process of returning to the church, it is important to help seekers move beyond their old understanding of confession. This transition is key to permanent reconciliation with the church. Those who come to us with pain, anger, and hurt feelings need to experience God's healing. Properly understood, this sacrament becomes a significant turning point in any journey of reconciliation. For those who do reconcile, it is a process that will continue throughout their lifetimes. Every effort should be made to help the seekers develop a new understanding of this sacrament. This may include inviting them into the reconciliation room itself, where they can sit while discussing questions and observations, or an invitation to a communal service of reconciliation, where they can make the choice to participate or merely observe. We have found role playing helpful in relieving seekers of those awkward feelings about not knowing what to do or say when they are ready to participate in the sacrament again.

For many, those negative memories are a strong impediment to returning to this sacrament and, therefore, to the church. We state the following very clearly to anyone who may be considering taking the "risk":

1. Not all parishes or priests have incorporated the changes of Vatican II in their celebration of the sacrament. Some still use the confessional; some still expect the memorized formula. Some priests may still respond as judge.

2. We recommend that Catholics should know something about the confessor. It is important that he be understanding, fair, and sensitive to the apprehensions or fears of the penitent. If you don't have a priest working with your team, it is important for you to have names of priests who are willing to accept your referrals. It is important that the priest approached by the seeker celebrates the sacrament

in a way that truly emphasizes God's forgiveness and healing.

3. We encourage our seekers to call a priest for an appointment, especially for the first celebration of this sacrament after a long period of time. This allows for a more relaxed atmosphere and eliminates the pressure of standing in line or catching the priest when he is already committed elsewhere and cannot devote full attention to the seeker.

Baptism

Seekers' Perspective

- "What kind of church sends a child to hell because the parents don't go to church?"
- "The priest said he wouldn't baptize our baby unless we joined the parish; it's just an excuse to send me collection envelopes."
- "They expect us to go to classes to have our baby baptized. Why do we have to go through all that before the church does what it is supposed to do?"
- "My baby died before it was baptized. Does that mean he is in Limbo?"

Church's Perspective

Baptism, together with Confirmation and Eucharist, are the Sacraments of Initiation into the Christian community. It is the celebration of our participation in Christ's death and resurrection, and the sacrament through which we become converted to Jesus Christ in a new way. We are freed from original sin and are called by the community of believers to participate fully and actively in Christ's mission of preaching and living God's good news. We fulfill that mission by our participation and membership in the church.

Vatican II stressed that not only does baptism free us from our original sinfulness, but it also unites us in a very particular way with the church. Therefore it is the initiation rite that pledges the new Christian to the community and to Christ. Prior to this broadened focus of baptism, all Catholics were instructed to present their newborn infants to the church for baptism. Church teaching indicated that children who died before reception of this sacrament would spend eternity in a place called Limbo. (Today the church recognizes that there is no theological certainty about Limbo.) Having a child baptized as soon as possible assured a child of salvation.

While many Catholics still express these same concerns about Limbo and original sin, the church has moved beyond this narrow vision of baptism. Vatican II has restored the original meaning of the sacrament. Sadly there has not been a good infiltration of this catechesis throughout the church, resulting in confusion and sometimes hard feelings among the laity. Also, there is diversity in how baptism is celebrated in various parishes. Some of this diversity is the result of the Rite of Christian Initiation of Adults (RCIA), the renewed rite for initiation of new members into the Catholic community. Historically the normal time to participate in the Sacraments of Initiation is during adulthood. While that may not be pastorally possible in all cases, some parishes may be asking parents of newborn infants to wait several months or even years before having their children baptized.

And, because the broadened focus of baptism now includes initiation into the church community, many parishes are asking that the parents of children being presented for baptism be active participants in the parish community. The rationale for this is if baptism means a child is initiated into the community, the child can only live this reality in and through its parents. Therefore the parents themselves must be fully initiated into the life of the local church. In some parishes, this is a prerequisite for any parents who wish to have a child baptized.

Pastoral Perspective

Most seekers are relieved to learn that Limbo is simply a theological concept without any official church recognition. We emphasize that there is no official certitude or church teaching on this subject. We also invoke discussion about a loving, compassionate God, who is steadfast and consistent in loving all of creation. It becomes difficult for seekers to reconcile a loving God with one who would banish babies from heaven because they did or did not participate in a particular ritual. Sometimes this concept needs to receive more attention than others. Some seekers are eager to accept what seems only reasonable — that God could love these children no less than we human parents. For others, however, this viewpoint seems too easy, too free of fear and control. For these people, it is the concept of God that needs more time and attention than the concept of baptism.

It is also necessary to help seekers understand the true meaning of sacrament, especially the Sacraments of Initiation, and how they involve the close, dynamic relationship of the recipient, Christ, and the whole church. Once we can leave behind the notion of sacrament as a moment of God's magic during which we are "zapped" by God, it becomes plausible and logical to understand the church's request for participatory membership prior to the reception of any of the Sacraments of Initiation.

Regarding stringent rules and arbitrary rejection experienced by some seekers who want to have their children baptized, it is preferable to set up some one-to-one time with individuals in order to understand the entire situation. It is essential that the seeker who is not ready to reconcile with the church does not feel that this choice is condemning his or her children to eternal damnation. Sometimes it is grandparents who come to us with this fear, wondering what their role should be in forcing their adult children to have the grandchildren baptized. In any case, those who are caught up in serious worry about this matter should not be treated lightly. If your parish has a preparation program for baptism, it might be a good idea to arrange a meeting with a concerned seeker and a trained layperson who can assist in the resolution of this issue.

Conscience Formation

Seekers' Perspective

- "The church treats us like children; we have to decide some of these things for ourselves."
- "Deep inside, I know what I have to do, but the church tells me I have to do something else."
- "The church has watered down all of its teachings by telling everyone to do their own thing."
- "All those teachings came from God; how can they be options?"

Church's Perspective

In aiding individuals in the development of mature Christian conscience, we recommend a pastoral letter from Bishop Michael Pfeifer, O.M.I., *The Freedom of Catholics: An Official Church Teaching.* It is a gentle but firm affirmation of the sacredness placed by the church on one's conscience and says, in part:

At the very heart of God's scriptural revelation and his dealings with humanity is the clear and ringing message that God has made us free. There is a hope in the Creator's gift that we should come in freedom to love God and to seek union with Him above all else. . . . The only love that God wants is a love that is freely given from the heart. No sacrifice, no rule-keeping, no . . . attitude can substitute, and no one else may force our decision.

If we are created so radically free by God, how can anyone tell us what to believe? How can anyone finally command how we are to behave? No one can. God will not, even though he awaits our free, loving response. . . .

The scriptures remind us time and again that it is God who is faithful even when the people are unfaithful; our own faithfulness is a reflection of God's. . . .

Conscience: The name we have given to that faculty, that place, that secret tribunal which God will not violate, and no other power can coerce, is conscience. Here is the place whereby we discern right from wrong in a spirit of striving to be faithful to God's natural law and the gospel teaching of Christ in the concrete circumstances of everyday life. . . .

Formation of Conscience: Since that is so, it is clear that our conscience must be well-formed, that is, knowledgeable and practiced, in seeking God's will. The formation of conscience involves us in a constant dialogue with God's scriptural revelation, with the ongoing tradition and official teaching of the Church. It also implies a dialogue with our experience and understanding of the daily demands which face us as individuals and as a community. Prayer for the guidance of the Holy Spirit is of vital importance in the process of conscience formation. . . .

God's gift of freedom entails the responsibility to seek sincerely after all that is good. The gift of intelligence similarly entails the responsibility to seek sincerely the truth in all things . . . freedom and responsibility cannot be replaced by authority in the Christian life. Official teaching cannot replace the responsibility of Catholics to seek the truth in those teachings and to give their assent to that truth. . . .

The Church offers its guidance to the whole community according to the best available resources at its disposal. One can always rely on this official teaching *at least* not to lead us astray even if a final word cannot be given. It is this assurance which obliges Catholics to open themselves up to what is taught, ready to give assent and obedience. But, just as the teaching is not final, both Church authorities and Catholics in general must be open to ongoing exploration and even revision when greater clarity emerges. . . .

Where does this leave the ordinary person? In all cases of non-infallible official teaching we retain the responsibility to seek truth and goodness in our own lives. Official teaching must be addressed to the whole Catholic world. For that reason it cannot take into account the specific circumstances of each person who seeks sincerely to hear the Church's guiding word and to live accordingly. The well-formed conscience will always strive to be based on the gospel principles of Christ, and on the best teaching of the Church. Prayer, study, reflection and consultation are of vital importance in conscience formation. This process should be followed before one would make an exception for one's self. But such a decision also implies openness to ongoing reflection and perhaps reconsideration in light of new teaching or new circumstances.[21]

Pastoral Perspective

When we share Bishop Pfeifer's letter with our seekers, there are usually two reactions. First, seekers may express surprise and ask why church authorities have been hiding this information from them. They want to know why they haven't been told about this freedom before. The next reaction is usually rejoicing. At last, they say, they can be adult Christians. Catholics do not, after all, have to practice blind obedience. Sometimes we actually hear sighs of relief. Seekers are encouraged by this permission to think and act and make decisions based on free, internal choice. This realization can be a turning point for many inactive Catholics. Because they know they can think and respond as adults, they begin to sense freedom from past hurt and anger. There is a glimmer of hope that issues and concerns can be explored, not through anger, but through a mature and realistic response.

But there are others who are uncomfortable with this newfound freedom. They have relied for so long on church authority to think and choose for them (even when it caused pain and hardship) that they feel insecure about thinking and choosing for themselves. They may confuse decisions of conscience with what is commonly called "situation ethics," choices determined solely by given situations. It is often helpful to assist them in discerning the difference between conscience and superego. Both are automatic instincts that we possess as human beings. Conscience is an instinct for choosing that is based on our need to be loved and accepted by other people. Normally, as creatures of God, conscience is used as the primary motivation for choice making. However, because human beings also possess the need to be in relationship with others, superego sometimes becomes the primary motivation for choices, especially when relationships seem to be threatened. Instinctively we always know which choice is the right one. We will choose right unless our desire for unity with others is threatened; then superego becomes the instinct for our choices. The difference between the two becomes apparent to the seekers and most would readily agree with these distinctions.

We do not encourage seekers to move quickly in this journey. We remind them that prayer, reflection, Scripture, and consultation are the primary foundation to any Christian process of conscience formation. We encourage them to become comfortable with these new concepts before they make new choices or decisions that will affect their lives, even those involving reconciliation with church.

Hidden Issues

We have attempted in this chapter to acquaint you with issues that are a source of contention between seekers and the church. But our experience has taught us that the stated issues of alienation may not be the only ones. Seekers may have issues that are not directly connected with the church, are more difficult to identify, and even more difficult to address.

John S. Savage, in *The Apathetic and Bored Church Member,* suggests that some individuals leave the church because of anxiety and anger that is not directly related to the church.[22] This anxiety and anger can be triggered by any event that causes estrangement. It can occur within the family, between friends, at work—anywhere and with anyone. The pained individual continues to live out his or her life, but when some church-related event occurs, the pain surfaces and is focused at the church or clergy. The individual then faults the church or clergy for not responding during the time of crisis. Usually there is a gradual movement away from the church as the pain becomes focused toward the church rather than on the initial cause of pain. Many specifically cite the church as the cause of pain, because it did not respond in a moment of great need.

We have found this to be true in our own experience with the seekers. It is easier to say that one has stopped coming to church because of confession or the hierarchy than to face other more personal and painful issues that are not church-related. Our role as ministers and facilitators is to create an atmosphere that allows personal exploration and reflection on these deeper issues of alienation. With free-flowing discussion in such a trusting atmosphere, the outwardly expressed causes of alienation often give way to the deeper issues, which may involve problems in the family of origin, lack of self-esteem, childhood shame, sexual abuse, personal or family chemical dependency. Because these issues affect so many in our society, the interaction that takes place between the seekers as they identify with one another's pain is often an important catalyst in the healing process. These issues are not always appropriate topics for the group process. For those whose issues lie deeply buried, even from themselves, or who dare not risk exposing their woundedness within the group setting, it is our job to offer gentle invitations to explore more personally the roots of their church alienation. It may be necessary to encourage professional counseling where they can receive the help they need in order to cope with these other issues.

For example, a seeker named Jack grew up in a home where his parents were continually arguing and where he was given very little security or affection. The church became the focus of his alienation because of his parents' strong ties to the church. In reality, Jack's estrangement from his parents is as significant as his estrangement from the church. The minister is called to help him sort out how both the church and his family contribute to his feelings of alienation and isolation.

Another example is Julie, who grew up Catholic and was taught that it was a sin to take pride in her own gifts, abilities, or appearance. Now, as an adult, she finds it hard to know a God who loves and accepts her. Julie finds it almost impossible to experience God's love because she is not able to accept and love herself.

Low self-esteem is a common denominator among most seekers. The church's teaching regarding sin, or a problem with a particular sister who taught school may be the stated cause of alienation. These may have been contributing factors, but with reflection it becomes apparent that the key to healing the anger and pain is a reassessment of one's own goodness in God's eyes. That involves scrutiny of many relationships, not just the one with the church. It may also involve resolving and reconciling relationships with self, friends, parents, coworkers, and spouse.

Most of these hidden issues of alienation are complex and require the proper setting for thorough discussion. This can be very time-consuming for the minister. However, if you convey patience, caring, and understanding, the seeker will be more willing to accept your invitation to journey toward the healing that is necessary for real reconciliation. This may be the first time in the seeker's life that these deeper issues begin to surface. Because the seekers are on a journey toward truth and wholeness with their God, the Spirit seems to bring forth those things heretofore unaddressed. We who are blessed to be a part of this process must evidence a sacred respect for the powerful effect the Spirit's presence has upon it.

Our discussion of these hidden issues as causes of alienation among Catholics is not an attempt to excuse the role of the church, nor to deny its responsibility for the seekers' anger and pain. Rather, it is a challenge to the minister to prayerfully discern whether a seeker is ready to search for a deeper truth that may be revealed in the journey of reconciliation.

PART THREE

Chapter 6

THE CALL TO BE A
RECONCILING COMMUNITY

Reconciliation is not a new concept in the church. It has always been at the core of our existence as a people committed to the fulfillment of Jesus' mission. Real reconciliation is not confined solely to the "little black box" or the Sacrament of Reconciliation. Rather, as described by Monika Hellwig, ". . . continuing reconciliation, sacramental in a broad and true sense, is happening in people's kitchens, and family rooms, and bedrooms, on streets, in buses and where they shop, in offices, factories, and farms, in playgrounds, theaters and hospitals, on Monday, Tuesday, and the rest of the week. That is where the church lives and breathes and plays its role in the redemption."[1]

While the preceding chapters have focused on the seekers and their process of reconciliation, the underlying experience of alienation and the need for forgiveness is familiar to all of us. Living in relationship with one another is also basic to our Catholic teaching; to be in relationship with God or others is to risk the pain of misunderstanding and isolation.

Reconciliation is the key to knowing the goodness in others and becomes the way in which we begin to experience the reality of relationship with a loving God. It is through the experience of genuine reconciliation that we become free of the burdensome concepts of God that stifle growth and our ability to live at peace with ourselves and in unity with one another.

We learn most about reconciliation during times when it is

most needed. When we bar broken people from our churches, we deny them and ourselves the powerful lessons that can be learned from the process of reconciliation. As Dennis Woods warns, "Those who undertake a ministry of reconciliation have to stay alert for those special opportunities that must be seized as teaching moments or moments of consciousness raising or recognition."[2]

Reconciliation does not happen automatically. It is not accomplished through any one experience or liturgy. It is a process that continues as long as there is discord in our lives. There are many ways for us as church to accomplish this spirit of reconciliation within our communities. One way is through the Sacrament of Reconciliation. While there is talk within the church about the limited value of this sacrament, we suggest a redirection of the focus of that discussion. Our concern should be directed toward the revaluing of the sacramental reality through renewed emphasis on living lives of reconciliation in church communities that reach out to the world, offering acceptance, forgiveness and affirmation of sacred dignity to all. Senseless conflict over which form to use, who is forgiven and who does the forgiving, will then be replaced with life-giving liturgies filled with the energy and power of the spirit of reconciliation already present. The sacramental integrity will be restored in the acknowledgment of the gift bestowed so lovingly upon us by our Creator through Jesus Christ, our ultimate reconciler.

Another way in which we experience reconciliation is through our celebration of the Eucharist. Reconciling parish communities have much to celebrate and they do that best in their Eucharistic liturgies. In these communities, mass is a coming together of people who experience God's love and forgiveness and need to celebrate that experience with one another. There are no walls or barriers, no judgments of who is "in" and who is "out" in these communities. Rather than a reward for lives lived within rigid rules, the Eucharist becomes a triumphant explosion of joy reflecting God's presence and power.

Finally, baptism calls us as individuals to be reconciling people. That call is characterized by a commitment to reach out to all who are separated from us. We cannot afford to sit smugly in our pews, judging others by old rules, measuring holiness with historical yardsticks.

Becoming a reconciling community calls us to a new way of acting, to a new way of *being* church. Bishop Michael Sheehan, in a pastoral letter to the people of Lubbock, Texas, described this call:

No more unfriendly, hurried coldness at the doors and in the pews of our churches, let there be life.

No more insensitivity to the prophetic teachings of the church on justice and peace, let there be love.

No more refusal to share with others the good news of Jesus Christ and the importance of his body, the church, let there be joy.[3]

It is our hope that as Bishop Sheehan's words become lived Catholic experience, our parishes will be transformed into reconciling communities, opening the doors to those who have left and enriching the lives of those who remain.

We are called to be reconcilers and to make our parishes places of life, love, and joy. Our efforts to accomplish this should begin small and be allowed to change and adapt frequently. In any reconciling effort, the focus must remain on the recipient and the message, not the program itself, and certainly not on those who administer it. In fact, the very word *program* can be indicative of too much expectation, too much direction. Programs often have to meet timetables, budgets, and human needs; these things can be stifling to the work of the Spirit! According to Monika Hellwig, our task as reconciling communities "... requires growth to maturity in faith in which judgments can really be made from inner conviction according to the mind and heart of Jesus and under the impulse of the Spirit."[4]

As our own understanding of the reconciliation journey deepens, it becomes even more essential that we involve the seekers in the development of our ministry. They are our teachers, our divining rods in determining our direction. They have forced us to rely more on God's spirit and to do less ourselves. Their maturity of faith and the judgments they make from inner convictions give evidence to the Spirit's presence in their journeys. We are confident that the Spirit will guide you, too.

In this spirit of reconciliation, we offer the following guidelines:

If you have a family member, or friend, who is an inactive Catholic

- Be nonjudgmental, affirming, accepting, and patient.
- Let them see your own faith working in your life.
- Share some of your own doubts and struggles with them.
- Love them unconditionally. (God does!)
- Don't push or force them into coming back.
- Don't argue about their reasons for not going to church.
- Do not place limits on Jesus' gift of salvation for all of us; do not question their salvation.
- Encourage programs and liturgies in your parish that will welcome everyone.
- Always provide an *invitation*, never a *confrontation!*

If you want to minister to inactive Catholics

- Do all the above, plus:
- Be willing to accept their anger or blame without taking it personally or becoming defensive.
- Take the initiative to identify inactive Catholics in the secular community.
- Reach out in a way that will respect the seekers' privacy.
- Become familiar with those issues that alienate people from the church. Check your own feelings about these issues.

- Take a good look at your own parish community. Perhaps you have people who feel alienated among your regular members. Start with them!
- Promote liturgies and programs that are sensitive to inactive Catholics and their issues.
- Be pastorally sensitive, compassionate, concerned, tender, caring, and reconciling.
- Ask yourself, "What would Jesus do?"
- Develop a catalog of resources: diocesan/community programs, counseling, support groups, and so on.
- *Listen, listen, listen!*
- Use prayer, team support, and processing.
- Consider joining, or forming, a reconciling team in your own parish.

If *you* are an angry or inactive Catholic, or if you are questioning the church

- There is hope!
- Remember that you have a right to belong to the church by virtue of your baptism. God does not abandon you as you struggle through life, not even when you fail. God's love, forgiveness, and peace are always available to you.
- Accept that love right now. Claim it, for it is yours.
- Seek out a place and means to express your anger and confusion; find church representatives who will listen to you, and who are role models you can respect, not just authority figures.
- It's okay to "shop around" on Sunday mornings. Find a parish where the worship and community feel comfortable for you, where you feel welcome, and where you can share *your* gifts.

- We ask your patience and forgiveness. As church, we are human: we make mistakes.

- Find a good *adult* religious education program to update your faith and theology. Explore the church's history, its constant change and evolvement over the centuries, and its reaction to and interaction with cultural influence.

- Start with one step; don't give up. Reach out and continue your search, no matter how small each effort may seem. Continue to grow.

- Be patient with yourself. Rest in God's love; trust the Holy Spirit to work in your life, to get you through the hard spots.

- Accept Jesus' gift of salvation—no strings attached.

- Comb through the Scriptures for the stories of Jesus that tell you about love, forgiveness, and your own goodness.

- Pray—for yourself, for the church, for all of us.

- Know that you are a part of our daily prayers as well.

In the few years since our ministry began, we have seen exciting, hopeful changes in the Catholic church. Most significant of all is the heightened awareness developing among individual Catholics that their lives have purpose and that they are very personally called by Jesus to build the Kingdom here on earth. It is this new life that calls us to continue on our mission to restore the Body of Christ to its wholeness. We believe that Catholic people are committed, Christ-centered, loving people whose increasing participation in the living church is at the root of its sacramentality. Furthermore, we believe in the sacred power of reconciliation between us as brothers and sisters in Christ, and the promise of that power to heal and nourish the entire church. We do not reconcile only to tolerate, but rather to learn from one another. Reconciliation brings us to heightened awareness of the Spirit at work in our lives as we grow closer to others.

It is in the universal sense of the word *Catholic* that we live as reconcilers within our church communities. The unleashed power of ongoing reconciliation forges together not only a people, but all that is good within them. Through reconciliation, fear of differences is replaced with new awareness of individual sacredness. Fear of weakness is replaced with dramatic proof of the power and strength of love. Fear of error is replaced with assurance of God's forgiveness and guidance toward all that is truth, all that is good.

We are grateful for your interest in the seekers, and invite you to journey along with us in this ministry to the Body of Christ. It is our hope that our combined journeys will bring us closer to a day when the church will be fully immersed in the sacredness of human life, reveling in and extolling the beauty of the human condition, thus revealing all that we can be, and revealing Jesus to one another.

Amen.

APPENDIX

A. Sample Visitor Card

VISITOR CARD

WELCOME to St. Lawrence Church! We are happy
you are here. Our "Friendly Family" wants to know how
we may serve you. Please fill out this card and drop it in
the collection basket.

_____ I am new in the area.

_____ I would like a priest to call me.

_____ I would like a lay member to call me.

_____ I have some questions about joining
St. Lawrence.

_____ Other (Specify): _____

_____

_____

_____

Name: _____

Address: _____

_____ Zip _____

Phone: _____

THANK YOU!

B. Sample Mailing Piece

Your Relationship With God Isn't All It Could Be?

WELCOME ABOARD!

Are you ....

Searching?
Confused?
Hurting?
Alienated?

You Can Find a New Relationship With Jesus & His People.

We Love You & Care Who You Are.

ST. LAWRENCE CATHOLIC CHURCH
100 Main St.
Anytown, USA
000-0000

— The friendly family —

A "WELCOME HOME" OFFER

You are invited to join us at Mass risk-free and see our Catholic community for a very special WELCOME weekend. Just open the door for a new love between you and God.

SATURDAY, NOVEMBER 5
or
SUNDAY, NOVEMBER 6

5:00 p.m.   MASS

*10:00 a.m.   MASS
(11 a.m. FRIENDSHIP & COFFEE)
12 NOON   MASS
8:00 p.m.   TWILIGHT MASS
*(*Free Nursery at 10 a.m.)*

AND . . . see reverse side for much more.

AN AFTERNOON OF FAITH RENEWAL

at St. Lawrence Church
Saturday, November 12
1:00 p.m. — 6:00 p.m.

Anyone is invited to attend any of the FREE Special Events listed below:

Opening Talk : 1:00 p.m. "Learning to Relax, Share, Grow in God's Presence"

Workshops - 2:15 p.m. & 3:30 p.m. - choose any two of the following:
- A PLACE FOR YOU IN PRAYER AND WORSHIP
- A PLACE FOR YOU AS DIVORCED, REMARRIED
- A PLACE FOR THE SINGLE YOUNG ADULT IN MODERN LIFE
- A PLACE FOR MARRIED PERSONS IN CHURCH AND WORLD
- A PLACE FOR UNDERSTANDING THE RENEWED CATHOLIC CHURCH

Liturgy: 5:00 p.m.

000-0000

- This phone number is your link to the *St. Lawrence staff,* who believes every person is worthwhile regardless of religious affiliations. We can connect you with any one of *40 volunteers,* who will listen to your story. These volunteers are from all walks of life: divorced, married, widows, some have families, singles, students. But we are all in one great, loving power: *THE SPIRIT OF CHRIST.* Feel free to test our preaching with our actions.

- A NEW WAY TO GO: The best and most popular adult instruction in the Christian Catholic faith. The next session, beginning January 7, 11:30 a.m. or Jan. 11, at 7:30 p.m. is taught by our professional Center staff. Usually 70-90 adults with an average of 25-40 attend. There is no obligation.

C. Sample Newspaper Advertisements

Welcome to our Family

The Friendly Family of St. Lawrence Catholic Church warmly invites you to come worship with us. If you are new to our neighborhood and you're looking for church — welcome. If you have been away from church for a while, please consider stopping by this weekend.
Come and see why we call ourselves FRIENDLY!

Sunday Masses:
Sat. 5 pm, Sun. 8 am, 10 am, 12 noon, & 8 pm

Weekday masses:
Mon. through Fri. 7:10 am, 12:10 pm & 5:10 pm
Sat. 9 am

Reconciliation:
Sat. 10 am, Mon. through Fri. 4:45 pm

Saint Lawrence Church

Paulist Fathers • Paulist Education Center
100 Main St. Anytown, USA
000-0000

We have: Bible Studies, Babysitting at 10 a.m., Volleyball, Religious Ed., College Group,

Coffee and Donuts, Adult Education Classes, Counseling and Much More. Call 000-0000

Marriage preparation, Instructions in the Catholic Faith, Men and Women's Club,

---

CONFUSED CATHOLIC?
INACTIVE CATHOLIC?
ALIENATED CATHOLIC?
An Easter Invitation!

If you've been away from the church, or are drifting away from it, if you've been hurt by the church, or are confused or angry because of your "Catholic experience," please consider this invitation to come and talk with us. Perhaps this Easter can be a time of resurrected hope in your faith journey.

Mpls. ★ **Two Locations** ★ **St. Paul**

TUESDAY, FEB. 28, 7:30 P.M.   THURSDAY, MAR. 2, 7:30 P.M.
100 Main St.   100 Main St.
Anytown, USA   Anytown, USA
call 000-0000   call 000-0000

Catholics

Inactive? Aliented? Retired? If you've parted company with the church over new changes, old rules, a marriage situation, hurt feelings, or any other reason, why not join us for an open meeting Thursday, April 26 at 7:30 p.m. at:

St. Lawrence Catholic Church
100 Main St., Anytown, USA.
Call 000-0000 for more information.

CATHOLICS

Has marriage, separation, divorce or remarriage left you inactive? Do you feel alienated or as if there is no one to listen? Why not join us for an open meeting Thursday, May 10 at 7:30 p.m. when we discuss possible options.

St. Lawrence Catholic Church
100 Main St., Anytown, USA
Call 000-0000

D. Sample Evaluation Form

EVALUATION

PLEASE NOTE: If you choose to complete this evaluation, it will help us develop our program. Thank you.

1. How did you hear about our program?
   ____ Newspaper Ad – Which paper? _____
   ____ Parish Bulletin   ____ Pastor or Parish Worker
   ____ Friend/relative   ____ Other

2. How long have you been away from the Catholic Church? _____ (OR) struggling with an unresolved Church issue? _____

3. Which item below has created the most difficulty in your relationship with the Catholic Church?
   ____ Marriage, divorce or annulment
   ____ Birth control
   ____ Pope, a bishop, a priest, a nun
   ____ A disagreement with member of the clergy, religious or laity
   ____ Lack of interest in religion – or in the Catholic Church
   ____ Changes: Too Many? ____ or Not Enough? ____
   ____ Poor preaching
   ____ Not enough emphasis on Bible in Catholic Church
   ____ Confession – Other Sacrament (which one?) _____
   ____ Other – Please Specify _____

(continued)

4. Was first Sharing Session helpful to you? Please explain.

_____

_____

_____

_____

5. Were the two follow-up Sessions helpful to you in your own personal faith journey? Please explain. _____

_____

_____

_____

6. Do you have any suggestions for our program, or special needs which we could help you with concerning your church relationship? _____

_____

_____

_____

(Please feel free to make additional comments below.)

OPTIONAL: As our program expands and develops, it may be helpful to have your name and address. We will not give this information to any other organization or church office.

Name _____

Address _____

City _____ State _____ Zip _____

E. Sample Worksheets

CHANGING CONCEPTS
OF GOD AND CHURCH

Prior to Vatican II:	After Vatican II:

Description of God

Judged Sin	Forgives Sin
Is Distant, Out There...	Is near, within me
Father	Parent–Mother/Father
Authority Figure	Friend
Hostile, Angry	Compassionate, Loving

Description of Church

Hierarchy, Pope, Clergy	People of God
Tradition	Scripture
One True Source of Salvation	Ecumenical
Black and White Truths	Pastoral Concern
Universal	Local Church
Structured, Rigid	Adaptable, Responsive
Rules to Obey	Informed Conscience
Condemning Sin(ners)	Forgiving Sin(ners)
Dogma, Law Important	People Important

My Personal Concepts

_____   _____

_____   _____

_____   _____

_____   _____

_____   _____

WHAT IS A CATHOLIC?

Circle the statements you feel describe a "good" Catholic.

Obeys the 10 Commandments
Goes to Confession Frequently
Goes to Communion Weekly
Says the Rosary, Makes Novenas
Wears Medals; Honors Statues
Sends Children to Parochial Schools
Does Not Worship or Pray with Protestants

Add your own statements.

_____

_____

_____

_____

_____

Is there a difference between a "good Catholic" and a "good Christian"? ____ Yes ____ No Explain _____

_____

_____

_____

_____

DEVELOPING A MATURE CONSCIENCE

Read each of the statements below. Then make a decision. Is the situation described a sin? If you think it is, circle **S**. If you do not think it is a sin, circle **N**. If you are undecided, or "it depends," circle **D**.

S	N	D	Killing a Human Being
S	N	D	Being a Homosexual
S	N	D	Missing Mass on Sunday
S	N	D	Sexual Intercourse Outside of Marriage
S	N	D	Abortion when a Mother's Life is in Danger
S	N	D	Drinking Alcohol
S	N	D	Smoking Pot
S	N	D	Premarital Sex
S	N	D	Divorce
S	N	D	Buying Ultra-expensive Clothing
S	N	D	Exceeding Speed Limit on Highway
S	N	D	Failing to Vote in State/National Election
S	N	D	Wasting Food
S	N	D	Smoking Cigarettes

NOTES AND RESOURCES

Chapter 1

Notes

1. Norbert F. Gaughan, *Troubled Catholics* (Chicago, IL: Thomas More Press, 1988), jacket cover.
2. Dean R. Hoge, *Converts, Dropouts, and Returnees* (New York: Pilgrim, 1981), 96.
3. Ibid., 131–32.
4. Ibid., 133.
5. J. Russell Hale, *Who Are the Unchurched?* (Washington, DC: Glenmary Research Center, 1977), 38–44.

Other Helpful Resources

Gallup Organization, Inc. *The Attitudes of Unchurched Americans Toward the Roman Catholic Church.* Princeton, NJ: January/February, 1985.

Haughton, Rosemary. *The Catholic Thing.* Springfield, IL: Templegate Publishers, 1979.

Greeley, Andrew M. *American Catholics Since the Council: An Unauthorized Report.* Chicago, IL: Thomas More Press, 1985.

Chapter 2

1. Rev. William McKee, C.SS.R., *How to Reach Out to Inactive Catholics* (Liguori, MO: Liguori Publications, 1982.)

Chapter 3

1. See Robert W. Hovda, "The Amen Corner," *Worship* 61 (January 1987): p. 73–80; Mark Searle, ed., *Parish: A Place for Worship* (Collegeville, MN: Liturgical Press, 1981); Eugene A. Walsh, S.S., *Practical Sugges-*

tions for Celebrating Sunday Mass (Glendale, AZ: Practical Arts Associates of North America).
2. Rev. Laurence Brett, *Welcome to Our Open House* (Washington, DC: Paulist National Catholic Evangelization Association, papers), 2–23.

Other Helpful Resources

Comiskey, Bishop James A. *The Ministry of Hospitality*. Collegeville, MN: The Liturgical Press, 1989.
Smith, O.Carm., Gregory F. *Ministry of Ushers*. Collegeville, MN: The Liturgical Press, 1980.
Brennan, Rev. Patrick, *The Evangelizing Parish*. Allen, TX: Tabor, 1987.

Chapter 4

1. McKee, *How to Reach Out*, 1–39.
2. Thomas Bokenkotter, *A Concise History of the Catholic Church* (Garden City, NY: Image Books, 1979), 433.
3. Austin Flannery, O.P., "Declaration on Religious Liberty," in *Vatican Council II*, volume 1 (Northpoint, NY: Costello Publishing Company, 1988), 802.
4. "Pastoral Constitution on the Church in the Modern World," in Ibid., 916.

Other Helpful Resources

Bellah, Robert N., et al. *Habits of the Heart*. New York: Harper & Row, 1985.

Chapter 5

1. Raymond F. Collins, *Christian Morality* (Notre Dame, IN: University of Notre Dame Press, 1986), 3.
2. John F. O'Grady, *Models of Jesus* (Garden City, NY: Image Books, 1982); Gerald S. Sloyan, *Jesus in Focus: A Life in Its Setting* (Mystic, CT: 23rd Publications, 1988).
3. F. Barry Brunsman, *New Hope for Divorced Catholics* (San Francisco: Harper & Row, 1985), 3.
4. James J. Young, C.S.P., *Divorcing, Believing, Belonging* (New York: Paulist Press, 1984), 167.
5. Pope John Paul II, *Christian Family in the Modern World* (Washington, DC: National Conference of Catholic Bishops, December 15, 1981), paragraph 84. All papal documents contained herein are published by the N.C.C.B.
6. Young, *Divorcing, Believing, Belonging*, 223.

7. Brunsman, *New Hope for Divorced Catholics*, 78–79.
8. Bishop William Borders, *Pastoral Letter on Human Sexuality* (Baltimore, MD: Archdiocese of Baltimore, March 25, 1987).
9. Ibid.
10. Pope Paul VI, *Humanae Vitae*, July 25, 1968.
11. Diocesan Development Program for Natural Family Planning, Bishop James P. McHugh, Director. 100 Linden Avenue, Irvington, NJ 07111. Telephone: (201) 596-4207.
12. Richard P. McBrien, *Catholicism* (Minneapolis, MN: Winston Press, 1980), 1025.
13. Pope John Paul II, *Declaration on Abortion*, November 18, 1974, paragraphs 11, 12.
14. Ibid., paragraph 26.
15. *Called to Compassion and Responsibility: A Response to the HIV/AIDS Crises* (Washington, DC: National Council of Catholic Bishops, 1989).
16. *Partners in the Mystery of Redemption: A Pastoral Response to Women's Concerns for Church and Society* (Washington, DC: National Council of Catholic Bishops, 1988).
17. Pope John Paul II, *The Dignity of Women*, August 15, 1988.
18. Collins, *Christian Morality*, 189.
19. Carolyn Osiek, R.S.C.J., *Beyond Anger* (New York: Paulist Press, 1986), 12.
20. Thomas Franklin O'Meara, O.P., *Theology of Ministry* (New York: Paulist Press, 1983), 208.
21. Bishop Michael Pfeifer, O.M.I., *The Freedom of Catholics: An Official Church Teaching* (October 25, 1986) San Angelo, TX.
22. John S. Savage, *The Apathetic and Bored Church Member* (Pittsford, NY: LEAD Consultants, Inc., 1976), 55–70.

Other Helpful Resources

Cunningham, Lawrence S. *Faith Rediscovered: Coming Home to Catholicism*. New York: Paulist Press, 1987.

Feider, Rev. Paul A. *The Sacraments: Encountering the Risen Lord*. Notre Dame, IN: Ave Maria, 1970.

Fitzgerald, C.S.P., George. *Handbook of the Mass*. New York: Paulist Press, 1982.

Fortunato, John E. *AIDS: The Spiritual Dilemma*. San Francisco: Harper & Row, 1987.

————. *Embracing the Exile*. San Francisco: Harper & Row, 1982.

Gula, S.S., Richard. *To Walk Together Again: The Sacrament of Reconciliation*. New York: Paulist Press, 1984.

Guzie, S.J., Tad W. *Jesus and the Eucharist*. New York: Paulist Press, 1974.

Hagberg, Janet O. *Real Power*. Minneapolis: Winston, 1984.

Hanson, C.S.C., James. *If I Am A Christian, Why Be a Catholic?* New York: Paulist Press, 1984.

Harrigan, James P. *Homosexuality: The Test Case for Christian Sexual Ethics*. New York: Paulist Press, 1988.

Hellwig, Monika. *Christian Women in a Troubled World*. New York: Paulist Press, 1985.

Holmes, J. Derek, and Bernard W. Bickers. *A Short History of the Catholic Church*. New York: Paulist Press, 1983.

McBrien, Richard P. *Catholicism*. Minneapolis: Winston, 1980.

National Conference of Catholic Bishops. *Economic Justice for All: Pastoral Letter on Social Teaching in the U.S. Economy*. Washington, DC: U.S. Catholic Conference, 1986.

Ohanneson, Joan. *And They Felt No Shame*. Minneapolis: Winston, 1983.

_____. *Woman: Survivor in the Church*. Minneapolis: Winston, 1980.

Priester, Steven, and Young, James, eds. *Catholic Remarriage*. New York: Paulist Press, 1986.

Ripple, Paula. *Growing Strong at Broken Places*. Notre Dame, IN: Ave Maria Press, 1986.

Schaef, Anne Wilson. *Women's Reality*. Minneapolis: Winston, 1981.

Weakland, O.S.B., Rembert G., *All God's People: Catholic Identity After Second Vatican Council*. New York: Paulist Press, 1985.

Zwach, Joseph. *Your Chance to Remarry Within the Catholic Church*. San Francisco: Harper & Row, 1983.

Smith, S.J., Walter J. *AIDS: Living and Dying With Hope*. New York: Paulist Press, 1988.

Chapter 6

1. Monika K. Hellwig, *Sign of Reconciliation and Conversion* (Wilmington, DE: Michael Glazier, 1986), 28.

2. Peter E. Fink, S.J., *Alternative Futures for Worship*, Volume 4, Reconciliation. "Reconciliation of Groups," Dennis J. Woods (Collegeville, MN: Liturgical Press, 1987), 37.

3. Sheehan, Bishop Michael, "Making Evangelization a Priority," Lubbock, TX, 1985.

4. Hellwig, *Sign of Reconciliation and Conversion*, 23.

Other Helpful Resources

Dallen, James, *The Reconciling Community*, Pueblo Publishing Company, New York: 1986.

For information regarding other ministries to inactive Catholics, contact the following:

Father Patrick Brennan
Office for Chicago Catholic Evangelization
155 East Superior Street
Chicago, IL 60611

Father William McKee, C.SS.R.
One Liguori Drive
Liguori, MO 63057

ReMembering Community
North American Forum on the Catechumenate
5510 Columbia Pike
Arlington, VA 22204

The Franciscans
Holy Name Province
135 West 31st Street
New York, NY 10001–3439

Father Alvin Illig, C.S.P. & Father Kenneth Boyack, C.S.P.
Paulist National Catholic Evangelization Association
3031 4th Street, N.E.
Washington, DC 20017

INDEX

pastoral perspective, 175–78; seekers' perspective, 173–74; views of, 175–78. *See also* Vatican II

Charity, 98, 120

Childhood experience, 11, 15, 17, 62, 107, 130, 131–32, 178. *See also* Religious upbringing

Church, as a source of pain, 21, 22, 24, 26, 35, 54, 64, 78, 132, 142, 167, 171

Church history, 52, 82–83, 106, 109–11, 125, 172, 198

Clergy, 6, 111, 147; insensitivity of, 29, 32, 54, 78, 140; member of outreach team, 78–80; shortage of, 80, 113–14, 146, 171, 178; preparation for, 120, 128; women, 171–72

Collection. *See* Fund raising

Community, 5, 12, 15, 17, 48, 102, 116, 142; church's perspective, 133–34; pastoral perspective, 134–37; pre-Vatican II perspective, 134, 135–36; reconciling, 193–99; responsibility, 161; seekers' perspective, 133. *See also* Fellowship; Parish community

Concept of church, 5; before Vatican II, 126; Vatican II, 7, 120, 126

Condoms, 166–67

Confession, 36, 54, 106, 178–81; and church dropouts, 7, 19, 188; general, 179; new understanding of, 180–81. *See also* Sacrament of Reconciliation

Confidentiality, 84, 88, 95

Confusion, 3, 33, 47, 51, 165, 197. *See also* Faith struggle

Conscience formation, 17, 31, 103, 106, 112–13, 184–87

"Conservative" parishes, 136–37. *See also* "Traditional" Catholics

Conversion, ongoing, 23, 79, 106, 108, 109, 112, 119, 120, 144, 150, 162. *See also* Reconciliation process

Cooperation. *See* Interparish cooperation

Council of Baltimore, 140

Counseling, 80; post-abortion 162–63; referrals, 77, 80, 115, 162, 188, 197

Death, 12, 17, 31–32, 37

Democracy and the church, 122, 123

Discernment, 47, 159

Dislikes list, 96–99, 103

Divorce, 78, 98; as cause of isolation from the church, 29, 32, 33, 40–41, 62, 68, 142; church's perspective, 140–41; pastoral perspective, 141–48; seekers' perspective, 139; traditional church view of, 54, 70

Dogma, 50, 122, 124

Dropouts: Glenmary Research Center study, 9–10; hidden issues of, 187–89; Hoge study, 7–8

Education. *See* Catholic school; Parochial school; Religious education

Ethnic background, 31, 36, 37, 40, 49, 129–30, 133

Eucharist, 39, 42, 48, 75, 98, 102, 106, 113, 116, 135, 141, 174, 194

Evaluation sheets, 102, 103

Evangelical Christianity, 16, 29, 45. *See also* Fundamentalist denominations

Excommunication, 140–41

External Forum, 145–46, 147

Extramarital sex, 149, 152; church's perspective, 153–54; pastoral perspective, 154–55; seekers' perspective, 153

Facilitators, 92, 93, 96, 97, 99, 100, 101, 102, 106–7, 122, 139, 176, 177, 188

Faith journey, 23, 30, 35, 56, 84; concept of, 10, 12, 115. *See also* Conversion, ongoing; Reconciliation process

Faith struggle, 25, 70, 71, 81, 114, 170, 197–98. *See also* Confusion

Families: change in, 67–68; and church dropouts, 7, 8, 30, 47, 69, 188; dysfunctional, 30, 68, 162, 188; religious life, 31–32, 36, 37, 43–44, 49–50, 51, 53–54, 115; stereotypical, 67–68, 98, 133. *See also* Ethnic background

Fellowship, 32, 46, 48, 116, 135